Assemblin

Peter Mullen

Edward Arnold

First published 1977
by Edward Arnold (Publishers) Ltd
25 Hill Street, London W1X 8LL

British Library Cataloguing in Publication Data
Mullen, Peter
Assembling.
1. Worship programs
I. Title
377'.1 BV283.S3

ISBN 0-7131-0173-3

Set in 10/11 pt Lumitype Garamond
and printed in Malta by Interprint (Malta) Ltd

To all my friends at Whitecroft School

Contents

Introduction

Why Assemble?

In an age when public religious observance is on the decline the writer of a book of suggestions for school assemblies needs to justify his effort. It is my belief that the traditional assembly—the gathering together daily of the whole school, year or other group—can be a happy and creative moment in school time.

Psychologists who talk about 'attention span' have been telling us for ages that what happens in the opening seconds and minutes of a fairly prolonged activity determines the subject's response to what follows. An interesting and lively school assembly can therefore set the tone for the whole day.

Moreover, if all the school or a reasonable section of it can meet in one place for this activity then the tone that is set might, with luck, stand a better chance of being of a unifying nature: a time when the school or group is conscious of itself as a unit and not as various dissociated pieces of a fragmented educational administration.

Procedure

It is best if assembly can be kept fairly simple in structure. Brevity, though often a good thing, is not the most important consideration. If you can capture the children's imagination you might keep your assembly going for fifteen minutes or so provided you stick to the theme. Though, in fairness to teachers and pupils, none of the assemblies in this book needs to take more than ten or twelve minutes at the outside.

So if the theme for the day is 'Popular Music' then anything not directly related to 'pop' should, as far as possible, be left out, or at least left until the end. It is preferable in this connection for the school to develop its system of communication about alterations to timetable, the venue of the netball practice and so on so that endless notices about such events do not take up assembly time.

If assembly is to be regarded by teachers and pupils alike as a cheerful event, then all the opportunity it affords for the occasional reading of the riot act should be resisted. If admonition is called for, a special assembly might be arranged at which the Headteacher could even reinforce the happy connotation of normal assembly with the introductory words to his or her castigation of the pupils beginning, 'Normally when we meet in this hall it is for a brief and enjoyable ceremony. However on this occasion. . . .'

Assembly might be made the proper time and place for praise—though even this should not be overdone since even congratulations to the rugger team takes attention away from the main theme of the meeting. But occasionally it does no harm to mention (at the end) some good work or other, a prize-winner, a successful concert, etc. Virtue should be rewarded.

The children should be allowed to sit throughout if that is possible. The leader of assembly should enter when all are comfortably seated.

How to Use this Book

One thing is quite clear and that is that schools differ widely in their practices and their needs with regard to assembly. Some have whole school assembly, some, by choice or through necessity, meet by year or other groups. The keynote of this book is, therefore, flexibility. I have offered over a hundred short talks on a variety of subjects. Teachers may simply read them out as they are written. Most are sufficiently generalized in form to be treated in this way.

Alternatively, the leader of assembly might wish to read the passage through first and use it simply as a thought on which to base a talk of his own which would perhaps be aimed at a particular age or ability level. Thirdly, he is at liberty, literally, to ad lib and/or omit whenever and wherever he likes. The talks are printed in simple alphabetical order by title but Indexes of *Names*, *Themes* and *Subjects* at the end of the book will help the reader to find something appropriate.

Of course, some schools have excellent performances by groups of pupils in assembly and this book certainly is not designed demagogically to displace these. On the contrary, perhaps some of the themes here could be developed into short sketches and other forms of mime, musical and dramatic presentation. I have no wish to teach any comprehensively well-organized grandmother to suck traditional eggs.

As to prayers. In our school the children seem to respond thoughtfully to a prayer in fairly straightforward language and related to the short talk. Long liturgical prayers borrowed from the Anglican tradition and the chanting of mini-litanies of versicle and response (e.g. 'Praise Ye the Lord'—'The Lord's Name be praised') alienate the pupils because these forms of worship overdo the archaic and totally formal approach.

But the assembly should have definite form and structure. Everyone should know when it is beginning and where it ends. *One* formal prayer often helps contribute towards this scheme. Perhaps teachers might find, as I have done over three years of taking assembly every morning, that *either* the Lord's Prayer *or* The Grace* said by all, answers this formal demand. And this of course should come at the end.

Assembly in the Multi-faith School

Some of these talks are specifically directed towards the festivals of non-Christian faiths: Hinduism, Islam, Judaism and Buddhism. But even a brief glance will show that none of the talks in this book is really meant to be informative in a straightforward descriptive way. My aim has been rather to draw out universal themes such as 'hope', 'joy', 'fear', 'wonder', 'humour', 'forgiveness' etc. from where they are to be found in the daily lives of the children

* The grace of Our Lord Jesus Christ, the love of God and the fellowship of the Holy Spirit be with us all evermore. Amen.

and to illustrate these themes by the use of stories and examples which are not limited strictly to any particular culture or belief system.

Those who wish to find out more about non-Christian festivals can do so by consulting the calendar published by the Shap Working Party. Also Ruth Manning-Saunders has produced a compact delightful source book, *Festivals, An Anthology* (Heinemann).

A Note on Music

It may be that your school boasts a virtuoso pianist in the person of the music teacher, an orchestra, brass or steel band and other aesthetic delights. If so, you will need no advice from me about the value of music in helping to set the tone of an assembly.

For those, like us, less well equipped may I suggest a selection of incidental music which we have found valuable. This list is of course in no way comprehensive:

Calming influences

'Symphony No. 6 in F'—Beethoven
'Piano Concerto in C K.467 (2nd movement)'—Mozart
'Requiem'—Fauré
'Clarinet Concerto in A K.622 (2nd movement)'—Mozart
'Symphony No. 5 (4th movement)'—Mahler
'The Swan' from 'Carnival of the Animals'—Saint Saëns

Lively tunes

'Violin Concerto No. 5 in A K.219'—Mozart
'Symphony No. 7 in A'—Beethoven
'Introduction and Allegro'—Elgar
'Concerto for Orchestra'—Bartok
'Also Sprach Zarathustra'—R. Strauss
'Country Gardens'—Percy Grainger
'Eine Kleine Nachtmusik'—Mozart
'The Four Seasons'—Vivaldi

Sacred music

'Mass in B Minor'—Bach
'Coronation Mass, K.425'—Mozart
'Missa Luba'
'A Ceremony of Carols'—Britten
'Messiah'—Handel

The children will always advise on suitable 'pop' choices!

PETER MULLEN

Absence Makes the Heart Grow Fonder

In time of war men must part with their wives and families. You've all seen those clips from American films of the marines, sack of belongings and kit over their shoulders, marching on board the troopship faces covered with brave smiles. And in the background wives and girlfriends, handkerchiefs at the ready, waving their menfolk goodbye.

Of course, everyone tries to put a brave face at these sad goodbyes simply because the first sign of real fear would start a vast lack of confidence—a complete panic. But how brave do the soldiers really feel? And what do their wives feel like having the knowledge that their husbands might never return? It's difficult to say. Human beings are very complicated creatures; as well as bravery they share many mixed feelings and emotions.

In a much less desperate situation boys and girls miss each other in peacetime when they are forced to part. If your girlfriend lives in another town and you can only see her at weekends, then Sunday evening is a sad time. All the week ahead before you can see her again. This raises awful tensions and doubts. Will she still love me? What will she do at the dance she's off to on Thursday night?

And yet there's a saying which suggests that temporary parting isn't altogether a bad thing—that it can even do us good. And that's when people say 'Absence makes the heart grow fonder.' Perhaps it does. Maybe it really works. A little parting, a little separation and the next meeting is all the more joyful for that. It doesn't seem to help make the period of separation any easier though.

In the last generation, some people have been talking about God's absence. They say the world seems foresaken by God. Science explains everything, but offers no comfort in the end because it has the knowledge and power to destroy us.

And where was God during the world war when millions were slaughtered? A loving God could not stand by and watch such massacre, so he has disappeared—absented himself. Man is left to his own devices. Human beings are on their own.

We don't really know whether this is true or not. It may be simply that sometimes human beings gear their attitude and actions in a way that is more readily able to experience God. It might even be that the twentieth century, horrific in parts through its wars and cataclysms, is living through a dark period of God's absence. It may be that we shall once again rediscover the nearness of God's presence and that this time of absence makes our hearts more fond.

Heavenly Father, help us when we feel that the universe has no purpose and that our lives are dull and pointless. Let us see that you are near to us always. Amen.

After the First Shave

There's a time in every boy's life when he has his first shave. Maybe with an electric razor. Perhaps with the old shaving cream and steel blade. It's not just like getting washed—far more important than that because it's a sign of growing up and coming adulthood. Shaving's not the only sign of course. In the old days, boys used to wear short trousers until they were about thirteen years old. The very first pair of long trousers was a real symbol of manhood.

After all it's about this time when boys start to notice girls—and you can't expect to be Casanova in a pair of flannel shorts.

Girls go through similar experiences such as the first catastrophic attempts at making up their faces.

You might think that this hasn't much to do with religion—that religious people encourage us to frown on the kind of emotions and changes which we undergo in our early teens. But not so among organized religion throughout the world. Look at the Christian church for instance.

It caters for all the significant times of change in our life from the beginning at baptism to the ending at the graveside. And it takes in marriage. Some people only use the church for these three events—hatching, matching and dispatching. But even those who go so infrequently to church recognize its meaning for them at significant points in their lives.

Well, what does the church offer for teenagers? There are youth clubs and that kind of thing but they're not significant rituals like baptisms and funerals. They might be very valuable in themselves and create a lot of fun and interest for young people. But the significant service which some churches offer to teenagers is Confirmation.

The service itself is quite an impressive occasion. The Bishop comes specially to a local church and boys and girls of about thirteen years old are blessed by him. They in turn make certain vows and promises of a religious nature.

But the real significance of Confirmation is its inner meaning. Boys and girls who've all their lives been in the care of adults, make a public declaration that they're now ready to take responsibility for their own decisions about right and wrong—about how they're going to live their own lives.

So you might say that Confirmation, like the first shave, is a sign of coming maturity.

Almighty Father, help us to take responsibility for our own lives, to make real decisions about right and wrong and to work out our future in the awareness of the needs of others. Amen.

Alkan and the Bookcase

What can you say about a man who was so fed up of people calling on him that he rented two houses in order to dodge visitors? More, that he lived most of his life in solitude and he died at the age of seventy-four when his bookcase fell on him? Perhaps that's enough to say about anyone. Most of us don't have a tenth of that eccentricity in our lives.

But there really was such a man and he was called Charles-Valentin Alkan. Maybe you've never heard of him and that wouldn't be very surprising because he's not well-known. That's largely because he died over eighty years ago, because he kept himself very much to himself, but mainly because he wrote the most tremendous music for piano which is incredibly difficult to play.

In his day he was regarded by many as being at least as good as Chopin and Liszt. Since his death in 1888 his music has attracted only the most gifted and daring pianists. It really does sound as if it was written to be performed by demons.

But perhaps the most puzzling aspect of Charles-Valentin Alkan's personality is his desire for total solitude. Why did he bother to go to the great expense of keeping two homes going just so he could be alone? It makes you wonder what it was about people that Alkan so disliked. Or maybe it wasn't that he hated people so much, just that he really appreciated being alone.

Alkan stands at one end of a line which runs between the chap who makes friends with everyone, is always going to parties and the like and the hermit. And of course Alkan is the hermit—or was for a great part of his life.

In between the eternal party-goer and the hermit are the rest of us. Some more outward going than others. Some more retiring than most. All of us need the company of other people. We all need sometimes to be alone. It would be marvellous if we could spend our solitude in creative activity as Alkan did. Who knows what masterpieces might be produced?

Almighty Father, thankyou for the company of other people and also for the time we spend by ourselves. Help us use our solitude to draw closer to you and the knowledge of your will. Amen.

All Around Sound

One of the most tedious jobs to have to do on a Saturday is to go shopping in town for a new jacket or some shoes. It's tedious for a couple of reasons. First, because it's such a drag to trail around town when there are so many other much more interesting things to do. And secondly, because it's always so busy on a Saturday and that means crowds, bustle and noise.

You know the kind of frustration this brings. There you are standing near the bus stop trying to agree with your pal to have a break from shopping and go and have a cup of coffee. Suddenly your conversation is drowned in the searing row of passing lorries. Your friend shouts in order to be heard, 'What did you say?' You yell back 'Pardon?' And everyone just gets angrier and angrier. How different to walk about the same town centre on Sundays when the shops are closed and the cars are all off disturbing the peace of the countryside. You can hardly believe it's the same place.

And in a sense it isn't the same place, because part of the identity of any locality are the sounds that can be heard in it. There's a real difference between allowing sounds to annoy and frustrate you and instead, listening to them with careful attention and noticing patterns and variations in pitch and volume.

Edward Cowie, a composer of music who lives in the north of England, has recently been advising people to do just this—to go out into your local town centre and listen to the many different kinds of sound you'll find there. He says the exercise is especially dramatic if first you put cotton wool in your ears and block out most of the sound, then take it out and notice the effect.

Perhaps you think this is crazy and not the job of a musician at all. Shouldn't he be at the keyboard writing music in a manuscript book or training an orchestra to reproduce carefully organized sounds? Well maybe. But it's fact that the apparently random noise of a city centre isn't so haphazard as you might at first think it to be. The chiming town hall clock, the stopping and starting of the traffic according to road signals and the regularity of human footsteps form the framework of a definite sound system. It may be that in the end you'll disagree with Edward Cowie—but listening, making the attempt on noisy Saturdays might make that shopping trip more bearable.

Heavenly Father, thankyou for the gift of hearing. We ask your blessing on all who are deaf. Amen.

Angels and Demons

What do you think about angels and demons? I'm not so sure, but I once heard a story that impressed me a great deal.

In a little town in Germany in the olden days there was a brilliant doctor. Not just a doctor of medicine. This man seemed to know about everything. He'd read all the large dusty books that scholars read. And he'd conducted lots of advanced scientific experiments. Now he was bored. He'd done everything. He was an expert in all areas of knowledge.

So one day he decided to conjure up a spirit who might teach him even stranger things. He got out all his books on magic and cast a spell. Soon the demon appeared. And the demon's name was Mephistopheles. Now the learned doctor had always wanted to travel back into the past and talk with the clever and beautiful people of the olden days. Mephistopheles gave him the ability to do this—took him into the past. But there was a catch in it. For in exchange for his strange services the demon demanded an agreement signed in blood by which the doctor traded his soul with the devil.

If ever Faust, for that was the doctor's name, should find a joy, an experience, which completely satisfied him then at that moment he would die and Mephistopheles could bear his soul off to hell.

Well, in the course of time Faust had many exciting adventures and he also did some bad things for which he became very sorry. But he never found complete satisfaction. He was always searching out new ideas, new adventures until one day when he was an old man with a white beard he found himself enjoying some quite ordinary task so much that he felt completely satisfied and cried out aloud: 'Stay, thou art so fair!' At that very moment he dropped to the ground—dead. And Mephistopheles came to claim his soul.

Suddenly, from the sky came angels with great beauty and power and might. And they snatched away Faust's soul from the clutches of Mephistopheles and carried it into heaven.

I don't know what you think about angels and demons and obviously the story was made up by somebody. But I think it's very beautiful really because it's about someone who wasn't perfect, who kept doing things wrong—but in the end he was rescued from an evil fate because he was a human being like us.

Heavenly Father strengthen and encourage our interest and curiosity about your world. And give us your help when our lives are not going very well; your forgiveness when we have done wrong. Amen.

The Angels of the Star Ship 'Enterprise'

You go along and ask fifty people if they believe in angels and it's almost certain most of them would say they didn't. And they'd argue that angels and spirits belonged to part of an old-fashioned way of looking at the world. You know—that idea of heaven up in the sky, hell down below and the flat earth in the middle.

Of course, most people won't object to pictures of angels in churches or on Christmas cards. And they won't deny children the pleasure of acting the parts of angels in nativity plays. That's quite acceptable—angels as part of a colourful festival. But most people put angels on the same level as Santa Claus—a harmless and pleasant piece of mythology. A fairy tale.

Now the word 'angel' comes from a Greek word meaning a 'messenger'. So in the first place these beings were thought to be messengers of God. Spirits he could send to visit the earth and take his instructions to men and women. Like the angel who appeared to Mary before Jesus was born.

But there's another kind of belief about these spirits of God—that they're there to keep us safe. And so there's the idea of the guardian angel—some invisible spirit who looks after each one of us. That's a very comforting thought for a small child to take with him to a dark bedroom. But is there more to it than just a childish belief? Are there angels who guard us?

Most people would again answer, 'No'. And yet look at the modern technological angels we create. In that marvellous TV programme 'Star Trek', with Captain Kirk and Dr Spock of the pointed ears, we see a whole star ship, belonging to an even larger star fleet, specially ordered to protect everyone in the universe. Now 'Star Trek's' only a science fiction programme. The producer isn't trying to tell us there's a real interstellar police force protecting us, any more than the makers of Christmas cards are out to convince us that there really are angels with wings. Captain Kirk and his men are like guardian angels. You might like to think about why people who've given up belief in the old-fashioned sort of angel still find 'Star Trek' so fascinating.

Heavenly Father, thank you for artistic pictures of winged angels and for the old legends and myths about them. Thank you as well for modern films of science fiction. Amen.

Apples and Atonement

You must have been in that unpleasant situation when you and your friends have been caught in some mildly naughty act. Something like stealing apples. And you know the inevitable questions that will be asked including that of an angry parent or headteacher, 'So whose idea was it then?'

And, of course, in all the best stories about children's exploits, one of the culprits—a noble figure—says with great courage, 'Sir it was me.' There are other stories where everyone tries to blame everyone else 'He suggested it' or 'It was Brian's idea, sir.' But we'll leave these rather cowardly versions on one side for the time being.

In the case where one noble offender owns up he might say, even more selflessly 'They had nothing to do with it really, sir. It was my plan from the beginning, truly.' And then in the best tradition of school morality, the headmaster, secretly knowing all the truth all the time, reluctantly dismisses the crowd, admires the confessing boy for his honesty and with a heavy heart and a light cane punishes him.

You may be surprised to learn that this is very similar to an ancient religious tradition—the idea that one person can be held responsible, punished even, for the misdeeds of many. In the Jewish religion on a special occasion called 'The Day of Atonement' one man, the High Priest elected for that year, enters the most sacred part of the Temple in Jerusalem—the Holy of Holies as it is called.

There he makes special prayers for the forgiveness and purification of the people. And he does this as an individual acting on behalf of the whole nation. Just as the boy who owns up squares everything with the headteacher so far as his guilty pals are concerned, so in a much bigger way the Jewish High Priest by himself atones before God for the misdoings of the whole people. It's a kind of reckoning, of putting right. The word 'atonement' spells it out for us really: 'At–One–Ment.'

Heavenly Father, give us the courage to admit our faults and also to forgive others when they offend us. Amen.

Arius—Top of the Pops

Some words have more power than others to strike boredom into the hearts of pupils. One of the most boring words of all time is 'history'. I suppose 'Church History' expresses more tedium than almost any other combination of two words. Church history—the very sound of the expression makes you think of drabness and dryness, of dust and decay. Who could possibly be interested in Church history?

Well, in the early centuries of Christian belief it wasn't quite as boring as you might think. Scholars were always falling out over details of the life or nature of Jesus, or about the date of Easter and things like that. So it sounds pretty boring, but it was the way they quarrelled that was interesting. Not in a quiet, professorial manner, but in a lively and rumbustious—often even a rowdy—set to.

The opponents would frequently gather a band of faithful supporters around them and attempt to shout down their opposite numbers. It was more like Manchester City versus Manchester United, Spurs against West Ham, than groups of scholars engrossed mildly in a discussion of technical points.

One such argument was between Arius and Athanasius. What they were disagreeing about might seem rather obscure to us nowadays—unanswerable even. But to them it was as important as life itself. Athanasius argued that Jesus had always existed in heaven with God, his father. Arius, on the other hand, said that God created everything, so he must have created Jesus. So there must have been a time when Jesus didn't exist—not even in heaven.

But the striking thing about this quarrel was that Arius put his statement to music. He said quite simply *ηυ ποτε οτε ὀυκ ἠυ* (hane potty hotty ook ane)—or 'there was a time when he was not', talking about Jesus of course. Then he went round singing it.

Perhaps all this fine argument around subtle points of theology means little to us nowadays. But the example of the wild Arius and his pop song might help to dissuade us from the idea that all history and particularly all Church history is just a bore and a drag.

Heavenly Father, help us to approach the task of learning with an open mind and an enthusiastic heart. Amen.

The Arm of Flesh

In most hymnbooks used in churches and schools there's a rousing tune 'Stand up for Jesus'. The hymn's all right if you can accept all that stuff about Christians being soldiers and the tune's probably one of the liveliest in the book.

But there's a line in 'Stand up for Jesus' that's less than satisfactory. It goes:

The arm of flesh will fail you;
Ye dare not trust your own.

A good case could be made out for saying that there's nothing particularly Christian about this line—in fact that it's downright unchristian. 'The arm of flesh will fail you' might sound like a good enough line for one who thinks you can only be a Christian when you're weak. But there is a sense in which it goes right against all Jesus' teaching about men and women.

Christian doctrine says that God made us, body, mind and spirit. So we can't chop off the mind and spirit parts and regard them as fine and good but then believe the body—or as the hymn has it—'the flesh' to be bad. God didn't give us good minds and bad bodies, but made us whole persons.

This isn't to say, of course, that human beings are perfect—far from it. But simply that God made all our different parts, body, mind and spirit to work properly and efficiently.

We may use our minds for solving all kinds of difficult problems. And our spirit may inspire us to great acts of creativity. But let's not forget the important part which our body—the flesh—plays. For a start we need the flesh in order to have the mind and the spirit. We use our bodies to express our care and affection for one another and to perform a great deal of the work that we do.

No, it's not that we're without fault. But we're more or less imperfect equally in body, mind and spirit taken together as a whole entity—a complete person. God doesn't want us to be weak, but to rejoice in the strength he has given us.

Heavenly Father, thank you for making us whole beings—body, mind and spirit. Help us to use the whole of our personality in your service and in care for our neighbour. Amen.

Atomic Puzzles

Atoms are very funny things. We might like to think that our century saw their discovery. We were the first to know anything about them. Well we do have the doubtful privilege of being the first folk to let off atomic bombs, but speculation about the nature of the atom was popular as far back in time as the Ancient Greeks.

Until very recently everyone agreed that atoms were the smallest particles, the tiniest bits of actual'stuff' we could talk about or even imagine. But then it was discovered that even the atom has parts—the neutron, the proton and the electron. That some parts of the atom orbit the centre of it as if in some kind of microscopic universe of their own.

Since then scientists have named other particles smaller than the atom—sub-atomic particles they're called. These sound even more weird with names like 'neutrino' and 'quark'. Makes you think that Dr Who's world might not be so unreal after all.

Even stranger problems emerge when we try to talk about just what these sub-atomic particles are. And this is because they behave in most peculiar ways. Sometimes it seems appropriate to speak of this behaviour as if the particles were microscopic specks of stuff—like miniature ball bearings. But at other times they don't behave like particles at all—more like waves. So the ultimate question arises, 'What are atoms?' And this is another way of asking the no less ultimate but more down to earth question, 'What is matter itself?' And the answer seems to be that we don't know.

Even more astonishing: sub-atomic particles don't even have the decency to behave in a nice, neat, ordered and predictable way. They fly about sometimes at random. Discovering this the physicists Pauli and Heinsenberg talked about a 'Principle of Indeterminancy'. Now that seems a contradiction in terms. How can you have a principle about something that's random? Perhaps it's because language fails us when we try to define absolutely the very nature of matter—atoms, the building blocks of the universe. And maybe words fail us because the created order has more secrets in store for us than the Greeks—or even we—imagined.

Almighty God, we thank you for those who wrestle with the difficult problems which arise for us when we try to speak too exactly about mysteries. Amen.

Bad Medicine

Do you remember the comic strips about Denis the Menace—the little rogue schoolboy? Always in trouble. For ever getting up to no good. I think basically though we're not supposed to dislike Denis. He's not really an evil character—just naughty. And he doesn't actually do really naughty things—he just gets up to pranks and practical jokes.

Of course he's a glutton. Food, food and more food. Denis can't get enough of it. A bit like an older comic strip character—Desperate Dan who used to eat cow pie. Now when Denis has been at the jam tarts, the cream cake and the strawberry trifle it's no wonder that he feels, to say the least, a bit unwell.

And this is where the medicine comes in, because sometimes the last frame in Denis' strip cartoon often shows him being given a spoonful of some awful stuff like castor oil. We know we're meant to think it's horrible by the way Denis pulls an ugly face at the first sight of the bottle. Perhaps you've had castor oil? Maybe it does taste foul?

But here's a strange thing. Medicine is supposed to cure us of our ills and perhaps it cures Denis too. But the comic strip leaves us in no doubt that the purpose of the medicine isn't so much cure as punishment—for stealing the goodies in the first place.

Now there are some people who believe that medicine's got to be nasty to do you any good. It's forced to taste horrible or it won't work. I'm sure these days there are medicines which taste of all kinds of lovely sweets and I'm sure they work just as well as the nasty stuff.

But perhaps there's a bit of a moral we can draw from greedy Denis and the castor oil. If we find out that the consequences of our doing something selfish and mean result in some unpleasantness—for somebody, perhaps ourselves—we might be a bit more thoughtful next time. Denis'll never change, of course. He's written into comics for ever. But that's not to say we can't learn from our mistakes.

Heavenly Father, when we cause hurt to other people by our selfishness, give us the will and the strength to say we're sorry. Amen.

Benjamin Franklin's Baby

The printer and writer Benjamin Franklin was well known for his support of scientific ventures and bold new experiments. Of course, some people have always criticized science and questioned the value of research into this thing or that. When the first hydrogen balloon ascent took place in Paris in 1783, Franklin was asked, 'What's the use of a balloon?' He replied 'What's the use of a new born baby?'

And in this reply Benjamin Franklin was saying something important and true about the nature not just of science but of all human life. In those early days of flight who could say with any degree of certainty what the use of a balloon was? No one then had the knowledge of the future and the value of aviation. Men—a few men—simply knew that they had to continue experimenting because they felt they were on to something important.

It turned out that their experiments and adventures taught mankind a great deal in the long run about flight, about electricity, lightning conductors, weather forecasting and a great many other things besides. But it was only in the long run. At the time of the first clumsy expeditions into the air a fair answer to the question 'What's the use of a balloon?' might well have been; 'Well it's useful in itself because it's new and unique. It's also useful because it has future potential.'

Notice how the same can be said of a human baby. We believe life in itself to be of value and we recognize that every new born child is potentially a grown man or an adult woman capable of playing a significant and creative role in the world.

Franklin's answer is such a good one because it brings out science's healthy optimism. Don't keep carping and asking what's the use—but press on, make the effort, believe in your original creative actions. Of course science has a dark side—bombs and shells; and so have human beings—sins and crimes. But this should not dampen our enthusiasm for new ventures, nor should it prevent us from rejoicing when new life comes into the world.

Almighty God, thankyou for all we have learned and benefitted through scientific experiment. Guide our knowledge, we pray, into the paths of peace. Amen.

The Biggest Explosion in the World

If you were asked which was the biggest and loudest explosion ever, you'd probably think straight away of an atomic bomb or even a hydrogen bomb set off in a desert test. You might think of some of those large tests carried out by the United States or the Soviet Union in the early 1960s. And you'd be wrong.

Because, believe it or not, the biggest recorded explosion mightier even than the hydrogen bombs occurred in Siberia in 1908. At that time, of course, hydrogen bombs hadn't been invented. So what caused the explosion?

Some have suggested an earthquake, but there are several good scientific reasons against this view. Others think it was a meteorite. If so, it would have had to have been very large indeed. If it had fallen on London instead of on Siberia, it would have completely devastated an area northwards over the whole of the midlands to Manchester and Leeds and westwards as far as Bristol.

Besides, one argument against the meteorite theory is that in the devastated area vegetation now grows at four times the normal rate. This doesn't usually happen where meteors land. It's more characteristic of a nuclear explosion. But as we know, there weren't any nuclear bombs in 1908. So what caused the explosion? We seem to be no nearer to a solution.

It has recently been suggested that it might have been the result of an atomically powered space ship. Crazy, you might think. There were no space ships in 1908 just as there were no hydrogen bombs.

'But', it's argued, 'what if the spacecraft came from another planet?' Even crazier? More like Dr Who than real science? Perhaps. No one knows for sure.

Before we dismiss this idea as lunacy let's just stop for a minute and think of the vastness of our universe and the thousands of millions of stars in it. And every star a sun. Some stars might have planets going around them. And if so, what about an inhabited planet like ours? Surely, the idea of life on other planets is statistically extremely likely. And why should we think we're the most intelligent life form in the universe?

It would be extremely arrogant for us to assume that we're the only creatures in the whole universe. And certainly swell headed to believe we're the brainiest. If the crash in 1908 was caused by a space ship from another world, what were they doing here? What would they have done had they not crashed? That's assuming they came in the first place. And, finally, might they come again?

Almighty God, thankyou for the wonders of your universe, for the sun, the moon and the stars. Thankyou for the great variety of created species. Help us to respect the world and to care for all living beings. Amen.

The Bilious and the Ecstatic

It's marvellous when it's your birthday. For one day you're the centre of all attention. Presents. Parties. Friends singing congratulations. It's all on for your benefit. This sort of rare occasion might give us a sensation of sheer enjoyment that's so strong and powerful you could call it ecstasy.

But sometimes at our birthday parties we eat and drink just that little too much. And then the next day we feel far from ecstatic. Stomachs rumble; faces take on a graveyard look and we feel really low. That's called feeling bilious.

You don't need a birthday to make you feel ecstatic. It could be anything that gives you joy really. A letter from a friend. An outing. A favourite programme on the television. And you don't need an upset stomach to feel bilious. The day after a special festival like birthdays or Christmas often leaves us with a let-down feeling. A sensation that all the joy's gone out of living.

A great English writer, George Eliot, once said that all Methodists—religious people like those who belong to the Church of England—all Methodists are either 'bilious or ecstatic'. She meant to have a dig at religion in a humorous sort of way. But what she says can also be true—not just about Methodists, but about any religion.

Our religious faith often gives us times of great joy—of fun and happiness. There's Christmas with the presents, the tree and the parties. Or Easter with its good news of new life. But there are other times much less ecstatic. Lent with its time for self-examination and the occasion for taking a fresh look at our lives.

It would be marvellous if we could be ecstatic all the time. Always on top of the world. Full of joy and fun. But life isn't like that; neither is religion. What we need to do is to use the 'bilious' occasions as preparations for the joyful festivals. For there is something to be gained from both.

If you like, our lives are landscapes. Sometimes we're on top of the mountain—ecstatic, joyful, everything seems perfect. At other times we're at the bottom end of the valley—miserable, depressed and not able to see much happiness. Feeling there's nothing going right and nothing to look forward to.

In these times it's important to remember that whatever we feel like, however bilious and cast down, things will take a turn for the better before long. And the ability to believe this and get strength from it is called faith.

When we see others, in school, at home or anywhere else, having a bilious patch it's our job to stand by them and give what comfort and hope we can. If we share our neighbours' sorrows, we'll have our part in their joys.

Heavenly Father, give us hope for the future and help us to comfort our friends when they're upset or worried. Amen.

Blind Faith

One of the main reasons why people think you can't be a scientist and be religious at the same time is that they think science is to do with measurement and experiment, while religion is about something rather vague called faith.

You know the kind of thing. Science deals with what we can see and touch and feel—the real world. It's about liquid in test-tubes and things like that. Real things like magnets and iron bars; atoms and molecules. And all looked at most carefully in the precise quiet of the laboratory. Science gets us to the moon, gives us radio, television and motor cars. It deals with the nature of the world as it is. Science isn't vague and spiritual. It's down to earth and true. And it works.

And then faith. Some people think faith is about belief in God and angels, in resurrections from the dead and everlasting life. About turning water into wine and causing plagues of locusts. Believing in miracles; that God will act in a strange way to do the impossible for our sake—to get us out of trouble at the last minute in a similar way to that in which the waggon train is rescued at the crucial moment by the arrival of the cavalry.

But faith isn't really about such miraculous conjuring tricks. None of the world's great religions expect us to deny our common sense and rationality and turn to magic. Of course, some believers do have a rather odd and superstitious attitude towards their religion and seem to hold to all kinds of strange doctrines. But the real meaning of faith is something quite different. It's not blind faith taking over when reason reaches the end of it's tether—as far as it can go. It's an attitude to the whole of life, and one that applies as much to the scientist as to the religious believer.

After all the scientist needs the faith that what he's experimenting with in his quiet and precise laboratory actually has something to do with the real world. If it doesn't, he's just a creator of science fiction or of interesting fairy tales.

And this is the test of the religious person's belief as well. He must see a real connection between what he believes and the world as we know it. In other words, if he believes in the eventual salvation of mankind he must be able to give reasons for his belief. Faith that flies in the face of reason and honest enquiry isn't really faith at all but simply superstition. Faith and reason aren't opposites but partners in the adventure of discovery which seeks to find out what the world is really like.

Almighty God, thankyou for giving us scientists and thinkers. For people who make tests before they say that anything is true or false. Help us to be faithful investigators of your world. Amen.

Brain Fever Bird

In a book about his own life Carl Jung the psychiatrist tells of once when he was ill in Africa in the tropical jungle. Jung was forced to lie in bed for a few weeks to get over his fever. Of course, it's awful having fever, a high temperature, a splitting headache and all the other uncomfortable symptoms that go with tropical illnesses.

Now it was made even worse for Carl Jung because of all the noises of the jungle that interfered with his attempts to sleep. And the worse sound was made by an odd and rare creature called the brain fever bird.

You can imagine all kinds of things when you're in a fever. But the brain fever bird isn't just part of a delirious imagination—it really exists. It's call—the sound that so disturbed Jung—is the perpetual repetition of part of a musical scale. 'Doh' 'Re' 'Mi' 'Fah' 'Soh' 'La' and then, missing out 'Ti' it goes back to 'Doh' again—and again—and again—and again!

Now that'd be bad enough under normal circumstances, but just imagine the torment of having to listen to such a tedious repetition from your sick bed.

That's an extreme example of the disadvantages of being ill. It's not always so bad. Sometimes when you're getting a bit better you can have some enjoyment sitting up in bed and reading quietly. Or listening to the radio. Having your favourite meals brought to your bedroom.

But for a lot of the time being ill is an uncomfortable and often a lonely experience. Even surgical operations for our own good can have a painful aftermath. And sometimes when we're ill we're left by ourselves for quite long periods. It's no wonder that we become depressed at such times.

So it is a good thing while we're well—in good health and good spirits—to remember those who are sick and to do whatever we can for them.

Heavenly Father, we pray for all those who are sick especially those known to us and those in the hospitals of our town. And we ask your blessing on all who look after them. Amen.

Sun. 17 Oct '78

But Not Just Yet . . .

People always talk about what they did over the weekend. Went to the match, to the pictures, perhaps to church, to a party or maybe just stayed in and watched the television. And the next thing the same people do is talk about what they're going to do next weekend.

In a way you can understand this sort of conversation about days off work and days off school. School tends to take up a lot of time on weekdays. There's the normal timetable, perhaps games at four o'clock and not much space for anything but homework between tea and bedtime.

But the weekend gives us all two clear days—so it's no wonder we talk about our leisure plans and look forward to Friday when we can begin to do what we want instead of whatever anyone else tells us to do.

There's only one fault with looking forward to something special: it can encourage us almost to live our lives in the future. And the only thing wrong with that is it takes away our enjoyment of the present.

Once a Christian man prayed, 'Lord, make me good but not just yet.' He prayed like that because he was having such a good time and he didn't want the fun to stop. Of course, the present isn't always enjoyable. Sometimes you might think it's hardly bearable. So looking forward to a treat in the future—like a trip to the seaside or a very special film—can help us when we feel a bit down.

But living in the future isn't really living at all. It's just making pictures in your imagination. The present—what another man once called 'The Eternal Now' is all we've got. Our lives are a lot richer when we try to appreciate what's happening at—as the Americans say—this very moment in time.

Heavenly Father, thankyou for weekends and other holidays. Thank you for enabling us to remember joyful events from the past and to plan pleasures for the future. Help us to appreciate the gift of the present moment. Amen.

By Any Other Name

In *Alice Through the Looking Glass*, Humpty Dumpty asks Alice what her name means:

'Must a name have a meaning?' replies Alice.

'Of course it must,' says Humpty Dumpty, 'mine means the shape I am and a very fine shape it is too.'

This is very odd because we don't usually think of names having meanings in the normal sense. You can't tell from someone's name what kind of person he is: whether kind and friendly, rude and unkind, a good footballer or anything else.

Of course, you can get books which tell you what ancient word your name derives from. For instance Peter means 'rock', Barbara means 'stranger'—as in 'barbarian'—Thelma means 'wish' and so on. You might like to look up your name in one of the paperback reference books.

People often have more than one name. Not just Christian name and surname. But someone called Sydney may be known as Sid by his close friends or as 'basher' by most people in the school—perhaps because he's always getting involved in fights.

God has always been called by different names. 'Lord', 'Creator', and 'Father' are just a few examples. And of course there are different names in different religions. Allah, Krishna, Rama, Shiva and many others.

It's interesting to note that the early Jewish people wouldn't pronounce the name of God. Instead they just used the consonants without vowels. They wrote the name of God as J.H.V.H. Only later did this come to be pronounced as Jahweh. And the reason they wouldn't call God by name was that they thought him to be so holy and heavenly that even the sound of his title was sacred. It might be dangerous, or so they thought, to utter the name of God.

And behind all this is the old assumption that to know someone's name is to know what he's like. Which in a strange way brings us back to Humpty Dumpty again.

Almighty God, your son taught us to call you our Father, help us to treat one another as members of one family. Amen.

Can You Only Be Happy if You're Good?

A famous writer called Aristotle once said that only the virtuous can be happy. Only if you're good can you find fulfilment. It sounds a bit odd to us perhaps. How often it seems that things are exactly the opposite to this.

Thieves and crooks and cruel or idle people seem to do well, while the good and the selfless and the kind appear to come off worst. Imagine someone wins the football pools—a quarter of a million pounds. Well he could surely buy a good portion of happiness with that amount of cash. A season ticket in the best stand for all the matches played by his favourite football team. A new house in the country, or an old house beautifully decorated and made absolutely comfortable. All the food and drink he liked—and someone to prepare and serve it for him. A brand new sports car. Loads of stupendous clothes. Records. Books. Pictures—anything in the world.

Doesn't this show that money can buy happiness, that being happy has nothing to do with virtue? Or take the school bully. He's happy enough. He can get anything he likes from the other pupils if he uses the right sort of threats. He can be as unvirtuous, as nasty as he likes and yet he'll still get anything he wants.

Surely Aristotle must have been joking when he said that only the virtuous could be happy!

But perhaps not, in a way. There was once a person who won so much money on the football pools that she vowed to go on a happiness creating orgy of spending. New houses, cars, clothes—anything you can think of, she bought it. She was divorced, married again and ended up most unhappily.

This isn't to suggest that she was unhappy because of her wealth, or that she was miserable because in some way she'd been naughty. It's just that money and possessions are neutral things. It's how we use them that counts. And that there's no short cut to happiness.

Maybe it's only by involving ourselves in some activity which stretches our ability and our willingness to give ourselves to others and to some useful purpose that we can ever experience true happiness. Perhaps this is real virtue. And perhaps Aristotle wasn't so far out after all.

Heavenly Father, give us the strength in body, mind and spirit to live and work for the good of others. And teach us the meaning of true happiness. Amen.

Chronos and Kairos Meet the Blood Donor

It's amazing the way that people are proud of things they can't possibly be responsible for. Things like their height or their hair colour—though in the age of universal hair dyes, anything is possible.

In his famous TV sketch 'The Blood Donor', Tony Hancock becomes very proud of the fact that he's got a rare blood group. No doing of his of course. You're born with a particular blood group and that's an end to the matter. But Hancock likes to brag about his rare AB negative.

There's nothing special about this except for Hancock's performance. It's his timing you see. There's a bit in 'The Blood Donor' where Tony Hancock, filled with pride in his own exotic nature, asks the doctor, 'What group are you then?' 'Group A,' replies the doctor in a matter of fact tone. Now after exactly the right length of time, the perfect dramatic pause, Hancock simply and only says 'Huh!'. The effect is shattering. Hancock so superior; the doctor defeated.

And all this comes about through timing. If Hancock had just said 'Huh!' without first pausing for exactly the right number of seconds the whole thing would have fallen flat. But he holds his breath for just long enough and the result is absolutely powerful.

The business of timing is an actor's skill, not something easily learned—more like a gift he's born with. The length of a pause isn't important in itself. It's how long to pause in a particular dramatic situation that's of utter significance.

The Greeks are able to describe this point better than the English. For while we have only one word for time the Greeks have two. There's 'Chronos' which means the ordinary passage of time as in growing up and getting old. From this we get the word 'chronology'—the series of events in time. And then there's 'Kairos' meaning something like 'the appropriate time' or even 'the nick of time'. And this is where Hancock excels in 'The Blood Donor'. He holds his breath for exactly the right length of time.

Timing is of the utmost importance not just in comedy sketches but throughout life. Knowing *when* to do something is every bit as important as knowing *what* to do.

Almighty Father, give us your help so that we may do the right things at the right time and that we may know when to keep silent. Amen.

Crime and Punishment

There have been lots of ideas about how to deal with crime. In the old days they used to hang people for stealing a sheep or a lamb. In our own time we're more enlightened—or at least we like to think we are—and so our judges and magistrates try to take into consideration the causes of crime and not just its occurrence. What, for instance, made this usually mild and placid man turn to murder? Why do football hooligans behave as they do?

The idea behind this new approach seems to be that if we can understand the causes of crime then we can go a long way towards preventing it. And the technique does work to some extent. There's much less crime in areas where recreational facilities are good or where the housing's of an adequate standard.

But in the end, if someone commits a crime, he's got to answer to the law. And, of course, this is necessary or we'd be living in chaos instead of in an ordered society.

Crime has a lot of different consequences, not just for society but for the criminal himself. He might be fined, imprisoned for years or merely bound over to keep the peace depending on the seriousness of what he's done. But you can be sure of one thing: if anyone commits a crime and gets caught some sort of punishment under the law will follow.

There's a marvellous book by Dostoievsky called *Crime and Punishment*. The main character, Raskalnikov, kills an old lady and steals her money. In the end he's caught and made to do hard labour. But the interesting part of the tale is the account of Raskalnikov's mind tortured by guilt long before the police catch up with him. In one chapter Dostoievsky describes a nightmare Raskalnikov has where he relives the old woman's murder. And that chapter is much more horrific than the one that describes the original killing.

Dostoievsky's point is that our own guilt over crimes we've committed is a far more terrible punishment than any that could be exacted by the law. The evil doing contains its own punishment—which is perhaps another way of saying 'Be sure your sins will find you out.'

Heavenly Father, forgive us for the times we have hurt and wronged others and deliver us from the choking effect of guilt. Amen.

Dali's Magic Piano

In art people know what they like. And what many people tend to like is anything that's not too unusual or shocking. For instance, most people find in the landscapes of Constable a real capturing of natural beauty. And the village scenes of Breughel with his tiny ordinary villagers please almost everyone.

But then we come to so-called 'modern art'. You know, the sort of picture you're not certain which way up to hold. The one that evokes the question 'And just what's that supposed to be?' Picasso, Kandinsky and many moderns come to mind.

There's one painter whose work doesn't contain puzzling geometrical designs or particularly weird shapes but who yet manages to disturb us and provoke us into thinking 'What does he mean by that one?' And that's Salvador Dali. His special technique is to go in for the odd placing together of familiar objects. In one picture he puts a chair in a desert.

In a great favourite Dali shows a pianist at a grand piano and on the keyboard he's superimposed six golden faces of the Russian politician Lenin.

The question is, 'Why do this?' There aren't any pianos with Lenin above the keyboard. And what's a Steinway Grand got to do with revolutionary political questions of identity.

Dali doesn't tell us. He paints. And really that's what art at its best is about—a direct telling in the language or medium of the artist something about the world as he sees it. If Dali could have told us what he meant by placing Lenin on the piano he would have told us—but then there'd have been no need for the painting. The point is that painting is the best way for that particular artist, Salvador Dali, to convey his ideas to us.

Art, and particularly so called 'modern art' is always trying to get us to look at familiar objects in a new way. Frequently we then have that strange experience of finding out that we weren't as familiar with those objects as at first we thought ourselves to be.

Heavenly Father, thankyou for painters, musicians and writers. Help us to look at new work with patience and the desire to understand so that we may gain more knowledge of the universe which you have created.

A Death in the School

It is a ghastly day when there's been a death in the school. Somebody we knew so well has gone from us. And we won't see him in this place again. It's very hard. There's everything to remind us of his presence. An empty desk. A name on the register teachers don't call out any more. What should a teacher do with that name. It seems cold-blooded just to cross it out. And yet in the end he must.

There's no escaping the tragedy and sorrow of death. Whether there is another world after this one or not is a question you all have your own opinions about. But death is certainly an end to this world. There's no dodging the finality of it. What then are we to do?

First, there's no need to be ashamed of crying. It's natural and it does some good. But there's no need to dwell on the circumstances of the death in a morbid way either. And out of death, out of grief and sadness comes something very positive and strong. That's because a healthy regard for the certainty of death gives us a more thoughtful and respectful attitude towards life.

Then we mustn't go over and over in our minds the times when we did something hurtful to the person who has died. Guilt and guilty feelings are only of value when they can shape our behaviour in the future—in other words when we can do something positive with our guilt.

What we can do and ought to do is to achieve all the practical aids we can for those immediately bereaved. That doesn't mean everybody running round to the house of —— —— parents and pouring out sympathy. It might mean sending a card. We can do this as a school. And if the headteacher finds there is real need for practical help he or she will let you know in what ways you can give it.

Finally, the blow of a schoolfriend's death can help us to treasure our companionship and to care for one another with more sincerity and strength.

Heavenly Father, give strength and comfort to those who mourn the death of a child. And help us to hold fast the hope of everlasting life. Amen.

The Dedicated Followe of Fashion

Do you know that you can pay £10 for a pair of jeans? Not extra-special, smart, good quality and long-lasting jeans, but jeans with artificial patches stitched all over them. This is because it's fashionable to look ragged without actually being ragged. Isn't it absurd, to pay a lot of money to look as if you can't really afford to pay a lot of money? And it's the fault of fashion.

By it's very nature fashion is always changing. It comes and it goes. One year it's long skirts; the next it's short ones. Wide trousers, narrow trousers, flared trousers, waisted trousers—and can you remember fluorescent socks?

The fashion industry, for that's what it is, is a very clever business indeed. Highly paid men and women exploit the universal fear of being left out. We all share this fear. We're scared of looking silly. So we obey the people who dictate to us what kind of clothes we shall wear, what sort of furniture we'll have and so on.

And to make sure they can keep on making money, the fashion people change the styles at regular and frequent intervals. It wouldn't do for you to make something—some item of clothing for instance—last you a long time. That would cut down the fashion designer's income. How often have you heard someone say, perhaps of quite a decent suit, 'Oh I couldn't possibly wear that; it's so old fashioned'?

Well it's up to you to decide whether you're going to be a dedicated follower of fashion or whether you're out to set yourself against the trend. Clothes are important, but they're not all that important.

But there are other kinds of fashion—fashions in ideas. And these are much more dangerous. It's one thing to cast off old clothes as unfashionable, but quite a different sort of activity to brand ideas and opinions as out of date.

Because, when we say an idea is old fashioned, often, without actually stating it, we're saying that it's not true. And that just won't do at all. Ideas are either true or false not in virtue of their age, but more likely because of what reasons can be advanced for and against them.

Many an old idea may be false. Then we need the courage to go against tradition and say why we're throwing it out in favour of a new one. But some of even the most ancient ideas remain true despite their age.

Which all goes to show that while it may be a harmless though expensive hobby to follow fashion in clothes, it's much more serious thing to deal in the fashions of ideas.

Almighty God, thankyou for giving us minds and intelligence with which to weigh the value of ideas. Help us to use our reason and not simply to be led by fashionable opinions. Amen.

Descartes' Doubt

There was once a Frenchman called René Descartes. He was a great mathematician and philosopher who liked to lie in bed until lunchtime. But you mustn't think he was idling his time away as he lay there. Not at all. In fact that formula you use to solve quadratic equations—you know the one that begins, '$x = -b$' and ends 'all over $2a$'—was thought up by Descartes one morning in his bed.

Perhaps Descartes' main contribution to human learning was his method of systematic doubt. He said that almost anything could be doubted—even the existence of our friends and our own bodies. How could this possibly be so? Well, according to Descartes, our experience might be a dream and any minute we'll wake up and find—goodness knows what—but we'll know we've been dreaming.

Well, can't you pinch yourself and tell for certain that you're not dreaming? No. Descartes would say you certainly can't, for if you can pinch yourself, how do you know that you're not simply dreaming that you're pinching yourself?

René Descartes tried to solve his doubts by locking himself away in a small dark room in order to see if any knowledge would present itself to him that was so certain that no reasonable man could doubt it. In the end he came to the conclusion 'Cogito ergo sum'—'I think therefore I am.' In other words, the only thing he could be sure of was his own existence, or rather the existence of his mind. Because I can think then I must really exist; that much cannot be an illusion. Something that doesn't exist cannot, after all, do much thinking. All the rest could be doubted. But the knowledge of his own existence he thought certain.

In a way this all sounds very plausible. But recently Descartes' theory has been strongly criticized by a number of philosophers. René Descartes has, according to them, made a basic mistake. He has forgotten that thoughts come in languages. If he can think, then he must think in a language. And if he uses a language—and he certainly did use a language to express his 'cogito ergo sum'—then he must have learned that language from someone else. Therefore, there must be other people. So 'I think therefore I am' isn't the most basic bit of knowledge.

It's not as simple as this really, and the philosophers still argue the toss over Descartes' argument. But there's a degree of encouraging charm in the argument against him: what we think, our language, and to a large degree what we are, depends on other people. We need one another.

Almighty God, help us to learn from those who ponder the deep mysteries of the universe. Teach us to think carefully and to argue with reason and honesty. Amen.

Disasters

In 1975 there were lots of films involving disasters. There was one about a fire in a large building—'Towering Inferno' and another called 'Earthquake'. You can guess what that was about. These horrific films were filled with the most incredible scenes of terror and violence. People panicking and falling out of windows from a blazing skyscraper. Cracks in the earth. Horror and devastation as thousands were killed and injured in the earthquake.

'Towering Inferno' and 'Earthquake', like 'Jaws', were immensely successful. Hundreds made cinema queues to get in and see them. It seems as if people take a delight in seeing fearsome horrors of this kind.

Why is this so? Aren't human beings basically kind? Don't they wish to avoid suffering and pain? When an earthquake or any similar disaster is reported on the television, everyone's sorry and sympathetic. People send thousands of pounds to avoid relief operations in the stricken areas.

Perhaps the reason for the popularity of disaster films is that we know they're fiction. Someone made the story up. Someone else cleverly filmed it to the accompaniment of loud and terrifying music. So it's not really happening at all.

But there are real earthquakes in which real people get killed and real towns are wiped out. And we do have horrible fires from time to time. Shipwrecks. Aircrashes. Floods and drowning. It's no use turning our backs on these events and pretending they just don't happen—because they do. And when they occur there's a spectacular element to them besides the human suffering that's involved.

It could just be true that disaster films are popular and that they serve a useful purpose. They give us the thrill of spectacular destruction without the pain. So like all good stories they're parables. They remind us that the world is a dangerous as well as a beautiful place. A place to be treated with respect.

Heavenly Father, we pray for all those who suffer in earthquakes and floods. Help us to take all the care we can to prevent accidents by fire. Amen.

Dogs Must Be Carried

You can have a lot of fun with some notices and instructions you see around the town. There's good old 'Keep off the grass' and 'No smoking'. And there's the one you can re-arrange and conjure with if you're travelling on a long bus journey: 'Please lower your head when leaving your seat'. No doubt you've tried this game many times and turned that expression into 'Please lower your seat when leaving your head'. It passes the time on long trips.

Then there's the competition that keeps young children quiet during tedious car journeys. See how many different words you can find for the loo. 'Toilet', 'Toilets', 'Lavatory', 'Ladies', 'Gentlemen', 'Gents', 'Men', 'Women', 'Males', 'Females' and, of course, 'Public Conveniences'.

Some signs are filled with possible nonsense and so are a great source of humour. The best of these is the one you find at the foot of escalators in department stores: 'Dogs must be carried'. Now you think you know what that means: 'If you have a dog then carry him up the escalator or else he'll trap his paw in the gap in the stairs'. It seems plain enough. But you could imagine someone hanging around at the bottom of the moving staircase looking desperately for a dog. Because you can't go up without one, can you? Doesn't it say 'Dogs *must* be carried?

This may be a rather absurb point which generates a little humour but there's a powerful message behind it. And that's the great difficulty involved in expressing yourself clearly and unambiguously. In this trivial example it doesn't matter very much if you misunderstand 'Dogs must be carried' and so hang around a supermarket looking for a puppy.

It matters very much though if you're writing a serious instruction or direction for someone else to follow. It is very important to get a clear meaning across to the other person. A famous writer brought out a book called *Clarity is not Enough*. That may well be true. But without clear speech at a very basic level you can imagine the mess in which we could all very soon find ourselves.

Heavenly Father, help us to speak and write clearly and to try and give instructions and directions to those who need them. Amen.

Dr Who and the Problem of Evil

Dr Who is one television programme that everyone seems to watch. It's been on for years now and about four people have played the part of the doctor and it's still going strong. There are good reasons for watching it. The idea of time travel and the utterly fascinating Tardis—an old police telephone box that's bigger on the inside than it is outside. It's treats like these and, of course, the confident, clever, humorous and mischievous doctor that make the programme a must for so many millions of viewers.

From among all the sinister characters who've appeared since this fantasy programme began the Daleks must be the ones best remembered. How many children have awakened in the dark of the night scared stiff in the middle of a terrifying nightmare about these evil beings? And then they've rushed back to the television the very next Saturday and remained glued to all future episodes.

Daleks—what an idea! Devilish computerized metallic voices crying, 'Exterminate', all seeing eyes and a steel antennae that shoots death. One thing about the Daleks is their extremism. They're not just moderately wicked. You can be sure they're never going to turn out as the goodies in the end. They're supposed to be totally evil. Absolutely bad.

Now this is a puzzling thought. Can anyone or anything be absolutely bad, utterly corrupt with not even the chance of even the tiniest bit of goodness showing through? The baddies in cowboy films often have a kind streak in their natures. Even Moriarty in the Sherlock Holmes adventures isn't completely wicked. But the Daleks, they're different. They're absolutely evil.

Perhaps it's only because the Daleks aren't human that we're allowed to regard them as utterly bad. Maybe this is the answer. Only a machine can be totally evil. Human beings, however wicked, always have some good in them. And perhaps that's because people can make decisions, can change and develop in a way that would be impossible for even the most intelligently programmed Dalek.

Heavenly Father, teach us to value our humanity, our ability to grow and change and make decisions. Help us to look for the good in our neighbours. Amen.

Dreaming

Once a boy dreamed a dream. In this dream he was at the end of a long, thin dark passage. And it was pitch black and silent as the grave. Suddenly from the end of the tunnel a bright light rushed towards the boy. It became larger and turned into the figure of what looked like a man—or at least the ghost of a man. With the shining ghost came the most strange, disturbing and haunting music. The boy awoke. He was very frightened.

It's very difficult to know what to make of this dream. Can it be interpreted at all? Do dreams have meanings or are they simply caused by an over active imagination feeding on a cheese supper? You can get books which make general statements about dreams. For instance, that they mean the opposite. So that if you dream you're dead it's a sign of life and so on.

Most serious minded people don't really think that books like these have very much to offer. They're a bit glib, like the daily horoscopes in the daily papers which divide people into the twelve groups corresponding to the signs of the Zodiac.

But a lot of scientists and psychologists think dreaming is a very important activity. Some sleep scientists have even set up a laboratory and they wake people up and ask what they've been dreaming about. It's all in a good cause apparently. These experimenters claim that dreaming is as important as sleeping. We need both for the sake of our body's health. And if you say you don't dream, the scientists say you're wrong. They reckon that everybody dreams; it's just that some people remember dreams while others don't.

It's difficult to know what to think. But it does seem a waste of time and mental energy if all those weird and puzzling pictures which appear in our heads while we're asleep are all for nothing.

Among ancient peoples, the Hebrews, Greeks and Romans all thought that dreams were very significant—that sometimes they were messages from God about the future. Think of Jacobs' dream about the ladder going up into heaven, or the dreams of Pharaoh about the fat and thin calves which were signs of plenty and famine.

It's up to every individual to make up his mind about the meaning of his own dreams. But you might like to discuss this among your friends and see whether anyone has ever had a dream which came true or one which gave some valuable information. You could even keep a dream diary recording every night's visions and see if you can make anything of them.

Almighty God, we ask your blessing on those who study the working of the human mind and we pray for all who are distressed in mind and spirit. Amen.

Entertaining Mr Hume

A couple of hundred years ago there lived a famous thinker called David Hume. He was very clever and wrote books about philosophy. But he wasn't very popular with the church because he was an atheist. David Hume didn't believe in God and miracles and things like that. And in his books he explained his reasons for his atheism.

But he was by all accounts a very witty and entertaining person: kind courteous and friendly. And a great conversationalist at the dinner table. Once Hume was at a banquet and seated next to him was a very proper religious lady who did a lot of good work for the Church. She didn't know who the man on her left really was. And all through dinner these two people of opposite persuasion enjoyed the most delightful conversation—much of it coming from the entertaining Mr Hume.

After the meal the lady arose from her place, and David Hume left the banquet altogether because he had another engagement somewhere else. The religious lady enquired of her host the name of the man who'd so delighted her at the dinner table.

'Ah,' said the man who was giving the party, 'that was the famous philosopher Mr David Hume.'

At this the poor lady was overcome with confusion. And she thought 'How could someone who was so kind and friendly—such a good companion—hold such wicked ideas?'

You might think the religious lady hopelessly biased and bigoted. Why shouldn't an atheist have a sense of humour? But sometimes we all tend to do the same as she did. We like to think that our friends are clever and kind. But do we just believe this because they happen to share our own opinions?

Prejudice, and all the terrible dangers that go with it, begins when people start to say things like, 'Oh, you can't trust him. He's a Jew (or a Catholic, or an atheist)'. In other words when we try to lumber a whole set of people with the shortcomings of one member of that set.

Our aim, which should have been the religious lady's aim too, ought to be to look further than the labels people wear like 'Black', 'Tory', 'Irish', 'Atheist', 'Catholic'. The individual is unique and important in his own right.

Heavenly Father, give us the ability to see each person as an individual in his own right. And help us not to make prejudiced judgements about others based on first impressions. Amen.

Epicurus' Pickles

About the last thing in Epicurus' mind when he was writing all his books on philosophy between 342 and 270 BC would have been English pickles. Epicurus was a famous Greek thinker who believed that all our knowledge comes through the five senses.

Now man's capacity to misunderstand his fellows is so astonishingly powerful that Epicurus' name has ended up on a pickle jar. It's not as simple as that of course. From Epicurus' idea that knowledge comes through the senses alone arose the belief, falsely attributed to him, that we should indulge our senses in fine and festive fare of all kinds.

Not that there's anything wrong with the enjoyment of food and drink, just that that's not what Epicurus intended when he talked about knowledge and the senses. But it so came about that people who enjoyed delicacies became known as Epicureans.

Delicacies now and again are fine things, but some folks think that Epicureans go a bit too far. These people are very careful and sparse in their consumption of food and drink and tend to frown on those who seem to carry a good time to excess.

You might say that this is a Spartan attitude towards life—an existence of discipline and self-denial as the way to happiness and knowledge. And you no doubt know that Sparta is also a Greek name for an ancient city where the young were strictly trained on a very limited diet.

There are all kinds of reasons why we shouldn't do things to excess. It's greedy; it makes you ill; and it stops you doing other things moderately. But there are equally good reasons for not going too far in the other direction either. You become morose and inward looking and unable to enjoy even the simplest of pleasures. Everybody knows somebody who makes a god or an idol out of fitness.

In the end neither of these two ways is really satisfactory. Both the Epicurean and the Spartan are fit for nothing—that is they pursue their lifestyles for their own sakes when really the point of any particular way of life should be rational. For instance eating delicacies helps powers of judgement and discrimination—provided you don't eat too many. Hard and rigorous training is a great thing if you're going to use your fitness *for* something. You might like to think which side of the fence you belong—the Epicurean or the Spartan. Most ordinary folk are a mixture of both.

Heavenly Father, teach us to discriminate, to appreciate good and fine things. And help us to share. Amen.

Examinations

Most of you will be taking a number of examinations in the course of the next few weeks. Is there a special way to approach these dreaded events—a way that will give the best chance of success? It's very difficult, perhaps impossible to lay down any hard and fast rules. Some people swot right up to the last moment. Others pack up all study about a fortnight before the first test and take a good rest. No doubt you'll all do what you find most useful for yourselves. Certainly it's a good idea to get plenty of sleep—if you can.

In the Lord's Prayer, the part that's often said in the form 'Lead us not into temptation' can also be translated 'Do not bring us to the test'. Or even 'to the examination'. For 'examination' is another word for 'test'. But the test referred to in this prayer is a moral test. A plea to God our Father, 'Don't let us be tempted more than we can stand'. We can't use it as a way of trying to avoid school exams, unfortunately.

But it raises an interesting question. 'Is it right to ask God to let us pass the exams we're going to sit?' After all, we ask God for all kinds of things in our prayers. For health, strength, faith, hope, courage etc. So why not a little prayer as we go into that severe and testing exam: 'O please God, grant me a pass. Amen'?

Suppose you've not done your best all year, but been content just to mug up on a few dates for history and a few equations for maths a couple of nights before the exam. It certainly isn't fair to ask God to co-operate with your idleness and lack of effort. It would be like asking God himself to cheat. No. We can't use God as a sort of miraculous substitute for hard work.

But if you've worked reasonably well and steadily throughout the year, it must be fair enough to ask for God's blessing on you in the coming test. That would be asking God to co-operate with your own hard work and perseverance.

Certainly a prayer for a calm brain and a steady hand is a useful thing if you're nervous. A relaxed mood is worth a great deal in the examination room. Good luck!

Heavenly Father, help us to face the coming examinations with a calm mind and honest perseverance. Amen.

The Exorcist

Some years ago there was a frightening film made called 'The Exorcist'. It told the story of a little girl who was taken over—possessed as they say—by an evil spirit. It was a very frightening picture filled with all kinds of weird and scary events. You weren't even allowed to go and see it unless you were at least eighteen. What can we think today about demons and angels? Those who produced 'The Exorcist' just invented the spookiest and most frightening episodes they could think of in order to take money at the box office. But where did the ideas of good and bad spirits come from in the first place?

In very primitive times, people thought the world was full of invisible creatures both good and evil. So the god of the storm was believed to be wicked and destructive; the god of the gentle breeze was thought of as good and kind. In a primitive, naked and defenceless world it's easy to see why people should have believed what they did.

Thunderstorms and darkness must have been unbelievably terrifying episodes to endure. How did early mankind, without clocks, modern science or instruments cope with the darkness and the cold? Only by calling that which was comfortable, good and those uncomfortable events, evil.

But what can we make of such beliefs today? We don't really believe that horror films like 'The Exorcist' are anything other than frightening fiction, so what do we do with words like 'angel', 'demon', 'good and bad spirits'.

Maybe there's a clue, at least one way of looking at the subject in the word 'spirits'. Frequently we say of someone who's down in the dumps that he's 'in bad or low spirits'. And if someone's happy and joyful, we reckon she's 'in high spirits'.

There's a line in a hymn by Sydney Carter which reminds me of 'The Exorcist' and also of the times when, for one reason or another we're in low spirits. And that line in 'Lord of the Dance' is 'It's hard to dance with a devil on your back'. Of course it refers to Jesus's crucifixion and all he endured then. But it also seems to remind us of the times when we feel utterly miserable and without anything to look forward to. As if we're weighed down by a great heavy demon.

Not a physical demon that you could point to or draw, but a weight which depresses us and makes us feel dragged down and depressed.

If we look for a good spirit to help, cheer and comfort us at such times, maybe we could think of hope as a high spirit, as a light spirit. Because it's hope that gets rid of despair in the same way that cheerfulness exorcises a glum spirit.

Heavenly Father, give us your aid especially in those times when everything seems black and there's nothing to look forward to. Give us the good spirit of cheerfulness.

A Festival of Lamps

It's odd to think of Christmas coming in October. Usually even the keenest among us hasn't started buying presents as early as that. But in the Hindu religion there's a festival which falls at this time of year. It's called Diwali and Hindus sometimes in conversation with native English people refer to Diwali as their 'Christmas'.

There's no Santa Claus in the Hindu Festival. And of course there's no celebration of the birth of Christ either. Indians have other prophets and teachers; different gods and stories about these gods. But like Christmas, Diwali is a celebration at the end of the year. The Indian calendar is different from ours though. At Diwali all accounts and outstanding debts must be settled and houses must be made spick and span for the feast. This is rather like our Advent—a preparation for Christmas.

Another name for Diwali is 'The Festival of Lamps' or 'The Feast of Lights'.

Now that's very similar to the Christian Christmas with all its decorations and the traditional illuminations on the Christmas tree. Hindus light every lamp and candle they can get their hands on and give thanks for life and food over the past year. In this way Diwali is a sort of combination of Christmas and Harvest.

It's a great time for children, the Festival of Lamps. They get presents if they're lucky and visit older relations carrying with them a lighted lamp or a candle. Perhaps the most interesting thing about Diwali is that it shows how two quite different religions, Hinduism and Christianity, nevertheless share many similar features. The careful preparations, the thanksgiving prayers, the presents and above all the lights.

It might just be that these similarities point to a truth that there is one God in charge of the universe but that different peoples and cultures call him by different names.

Almighty God, thankyou for revealing your nature to men and women in many and different ways. Thankyou for the lights of Christmas and Diwali. Amen.

Fighting and Fasting

The Moslem religion is in a way similar to the faith of the Old Testament. Full of exciting episodes and battles. Most young people like to read a good tale about a fight or a siege or a war. You've only to think of David and Goliath or all those escapades the Israelites got up to under the leadership of Moses. And what about that tale of Joshua and the walls of Jericho tumbling down.

But there's another way in which the Old Testament, Jewish religion is like the Moslem faith. Both believe in fasting—in going without food and drink for religious reasons. Not all the time of course, but on special occasions. The great Moslem fast is called Ramadan.

This must be a very difficult fast to keep—especially when according to the Moslem calendar—Ramadan occurs in summer. And that's because the rule of the fast is not to eat during the hours of daylight.

Well, what's the point of going without food when there's food on the table or in the larder ready to be eaten? Many people are suspicious of folk who deny themselves the good things of life. 'Holy Joes' they call them or 'Miserable Devils', 'Religious Maniacs' and worse names than these even! And that's because fasting and looking glum is often thought to be a way of drawing attention to oneself as if to say, 'Look at me. I'm fasting. I'm denying myself. I'm religious, I am.' And of course if fasting is done with that intention then it's hypocrisy. In fact Jesus condemned that way of doing it. 'When you fast,' he said, 'wash your face and anoint your head with oil.' Well, we don't go in much for anointing with oil these days. But it's easy to see what Jesus was telling us. He meant us not to boast about our fasting and self-denial.

This goes for Moslems as well as Christians. A fast is a period for self-examination and for prayer. For reflecting on God's purpose for us in our lives. In Lent or in Ramadan we can all cope with some self-denial without looking tortured and glum.

Heavenly Father, teach us that you are one God and that there are many ways which lead to you. Help us to learn from the religious experience of those other faiths than our own. Amen.

Football Hooliganism

When there's an important game of football—a needle match—you can often expect trouble. If the scores are level at the end of extra time and the referee allows a controversial goal, the losing side's supporters are liable to become very angry. As we know, they've frequently rushed onto the pitch and games have been held up or even abandoned because of this.

And it's not just this so called 'football hooliganism' that sets people grumbling about violence. There's mugging and racial thuggery besides a great deal of destruction of property for no apparent reason.

If you ask why there's so much trouble, some folks will give you an answer which isn't really an answer at all. 'Ah,' they'll say, 'there's a lot more violence about these days.' What can this possibly mean—a lot more violence about—as though it's something in the air or in the water supply? Or as if it's like saying 'There have been a lot more ladybirds about this summer.'

Can it really be that human beings have changed so much in such a short time? Are we all really vastly more destructive and aggressive now than we were half a century ago? That's what a lot of people in their fifties and sixties would have us believe. As though the present generation has declined, corrupted and gone to the dogs.

It may be a good idea to remind those who tell us we're all that much more violent nowadays, that only a generation ago almost every nation on earth was engaged in the most violent conflict of all time—the second world war. Guns, planes, bombs, tanks and submarines.

'Ah, but,' they'll say, 'that was for a purpose. Hitler had to be stopped. The freedom of the world was at stake.' And, in a way, they're quite right. Not just about the war but perhaps about violence as well.

Maybe human beings are pretty violent creatures. Sometimes our aggression finds an outlet as in the case of an officially sanctioned war. It's no use being in a war if you're not capable of aggression.

Does this point to the dismal conclusion to the effect that we need wars in order to get rid of our violent tendencies? Wars are after all terrible events which must surely be avoided whenever possible. But perhaps it's not the war that's important but the purpose, the sense of direction and of being part of a cause that we really need. Perhaps it's not so much that there's more violence about but that there's more purposelessness about. Maybe we need to find more causes for which we're prepared to stand out.

Almighty God, we pray for peace and justice and we ask your guidance for when we have to decide on which occasions we should be justly angry and when we should keep silent. Amen.

Geriatric Prodigies

You've probably heard those famous theories about astonishing achievements by children. Mozart for instance, was writing music by the time he was four years old. And he'd heard his first opera performed before he reached the age of thirteen. There's a name for such amazing childhood genius. They're called 'child prodigies.' People like Mozart baffle us because we can't imagine where they got their knowledge from. Some people believe quite simply that they were born with it.

In the same way many other young people are outstanding at chess or ball games from a very early age. It's very difficult to account for this triumph of untrained genius.

But here's an interesting fact. A few rare individuals enter their most creative period when they're quite old. The German poet, Wolfgang Goethe, wrote his greatest work *Faust* over a period of more than sixty years. He put the final touches to it when he was in his eighties.

George Bernard Shaw, the humourist and playwright, was still turning out work of a high standard well into his old age. Bertrand Russell published his *History of Western Philosophy* when he was in his seventies.

Perhaps the most amazing character among recent old age genius was Havergal Brian. He was a musician and composer. After the age of seventy-eight when most folk are quite happy to take to the slippers and the fireside, Havergal Brian wrote another twenty-three symphonies. Thanks to another musician called Robert Simpson these interesting pieces are now being played on the radio. Some of them Havergal Brian hadn't even heard before he died at the ripe old age of ninety-six.

Now our society so obviously worships youth. Look at all the advertisements on the television. They nearly always feature the young and beautiful with the implication that if we only eat so and so or drink such and such we can be as desirable as these screen gods and goddesses.

Not every old person is as creative and powerful as Havergal Brian. Even most young people don't have a quarter of the energy and inspiration of this great old composer. But what these artists on the pension—these geriatric prodigies—ought to teach us is that old age isn't simply an ebbing away, a weakening and a dying off. It's a time of life that can be extremely productive. When we're tempted to write off old people as 'past it'—we should remember Havergal Brian.

Heavenly Father, help us not to ignore the wisdom of old age, but teach us to accept the frailty of our grandparents and to be prepared to learn from them. Amen.

Gershwin's Dead

Someone once broke the news of the death of a famous and greatly loved composer of popular music. And this is what he said: 'Gershwin's dead, but you don't have to believe it.' Whatever could he have meant by such a strange saying? 'Gershwin's dead . . . but you don't have to believe it'?

Either the man was dead or he was alive. Surely that odd announcement of his death was some kind of cruel joke. Something in bad taste.

There is a way of looking at it though that makes a peculiar kind of sense. What if the bringer of the bad news was really trying to say 'Look the man George Gershwin has died but in one way it doesn't make us sad because we still have all his wonderful tunes and nobody can take those away. They're eternal.'

Some people think we can look at the resurrection of Jesus in the same way. A lot of folk find it impossible to believe in all those stories about the empty tomb and the stone being rolled away. The incidents involving angels and folded grave clothes seem pure fantasy.

But maybe we can look at the life of the disciples immediately after the crucifixion and then look again a little later. They were changed men. One day downcast and miserable, their friend and master violently taken from them and put to agonizing death. The next day there were ecstatic, running out into the street and shouting to everyone the good news of the resurrection.

Now it's up to you to make up your own mind about what happened to Jesus after his death. Perhaps he did rise again. Certainly many people believe he did. But if he didn't something must have happened. How else were the disciples changed from brokenhearted and frightened men into joyful confident messengers of good news?

The question is very baffling. But when we look at the new life in those men and women who were Christ's first followers, we might say: 'Jesus is dead, but you don't have to believe it.'

Heavenly Father, fill us with the joyful life which was shared by your son's first followers. The life they called 'resurrection'. Amen.

The Glass Bead Game

Hermann Hesse wrote many novels. But by general consent his greatest is called *The Glass Bead Game.* It's a large work and so not one that can be fully described in a few minutes. If we can try to select one theme from it in this short time it must be the idea of withdrawal from the everyday world into a rarified atmosphere of pure thought and meditation.

Castalia is a province populated and ruled by exceedingly clever men. They have left the concerns of the day to day world in order to pursue knowledge and wisdom as far as they can. Naturally the training for such an occupation is very arduous. Each student learns to pursue one particular art such as mathematics or music to a high level of attainment. Then he is taught the skill of meditation and reflective silence.

Only then is he ready for the supreme mental exercise—participation in the Glass Bead Games. Hesse nowhere says what exactly are the rules of this game. But it's like playing chess with ideas, references and musical tunes in place of chessmen. All Castalians learn the game but not all become proficient at it. The supreme player is elected by an élite of intellectuals and given the little Magister Ludi—Master of the Glass Bead Game. He's a bit like a king, and a little like a high priest. The Magister Ludi's Job is to supervize the growth and development of the up and coming students and to ensure that the high standards of the province are maintained.

Castalia has little connection with the outside world. Its students are rather like monks who've taken a vow to keep themselves at a distance from the commonplace. The disciplined pursuit of wisdom is regarded as the highest good.

It's not spoiling the novel for you to say what Hermann Hesse is really asking is 'Can a creamed-off, distinct, intellectual and spiritual élite, by themselves and given time, attain true wisdom?' It would ruin the novel to spell out in detail Hesse's conclusion. So maybe it might be a good thing just to leave the question with you. Do we learn better through having a connection with the everyday world, or would we be more able to pursue excellence in an atmosphere removed from all other obligations and distractions?

Heavenly Father, help us in our studies. Teach us how to gain wisdom and knowledge. And help us to relate what we learn to the way we live with one another. Amen.

God's Advertisements

What do you think about saints? If you go to almost any church you'll see pictures and perhaps even statues of saints. They're in the stained glass windows as well. In some people's minds saints stand for all that's 'goody-goody', a kind of soppy, soft holiness. But this doesn't fit the facts of what we know about saints at all.

Take St Paul, for instance. Read any of his letters in the New Testament and you won't find a soft 'goody-goody do-gooder' there. Paul was always getting angry with people when they became stubborn and perverse. He wasn't afraid to shout, to grumble and to complain. And Paul was a tough guy too. He'd never have survived all the beatings and floggings he received otherwise.

And some think saints to be quiet characters without fire and passion. You can't read the life of St Augustine and still believe that. He was the one who was having such a wild time that he prayed, 'Lord make me good, but not just yet.'

St Joan isn't remembered for her peaceful contribution to the development of the human spirit either. Peter, we know was a fiery character—temperamental and passionate.

Of course there are saints who are revered for their quietness and peace. We can think of St Francis or of St John. But they're not necessarily in a majority. God, when he asks us to follow him, doesn't wish to squash all the strengths in our personality, but to encourage us to use those strengths in the cause he intends. God has no desire to calm us down if we're naturally lively, nor perhaps to turn us into raving maniacs for the Gospel's sake if we're normally quiet and peaceful individuals.

But we should aim to develop our strengths to the limit of our potential all the while seeking to understand ourselves more fully and to put our personalities to a proper use in the light of that understanding. God wants us to become great for him. We're all called to be what the saints are—different human expressions of personal qualities in the service of God. If you like, you could call the saints 'God's advertisements'.

Heavenly Father, thank you for the lives of the saints and for their examples to us. Help us to develop our own gifts in your service. Amen.

The Golliwog on the Jam Jar

There's a kind of jam you can buy with a label which pictures a golliwog. And the golliwog is holding a jar of jam and on that jar there's a picture of a golliwog holding a jar of jam and so on for ever. You can't see the labels after a while of course because the pictures get smaller and smaller. But you're left in no doubt that the golliwogs and jam jars go on for eternity.

This is a bit like halving a half. You get a quarter, an eighth, a sixteenth etc. but you can never get to nothing. Or it's similar to the chicken and the egg. The egg comes from the chicken which was hatched from the egg which came from a chicken and so on and so on for all time.

These three examples, the golliwogs, the numbers and the chickens have one thing in common. They're examples of what's called an infinite regress—a going back forever.

Now some people believe in God so that they can escape from the uncomfortable idea that the universe is an infinite regress. You know the kind of argument:

'Who made me?'
'Your parents.'
'Who made my parents?'
'Your grandparents.'
'Who made them?'
'Well they and their ancestors gradually evolved from primitive life forms.'
'So who made the primitive life forms?'
'They developed from the inorganic matter that formed the pre-historic world.'
'And where did this world come from?'
'From clouds of hydrogen gas.'
'And where did the hydrogen gas come from?'
'Ah well I suppose God . . .'

And the speaker might go on to argue the existence of God as a way of getting out of an infinite regress. The trouble is that people can, and often do, ask 'But who made God?'. Then there's a puzzle when it's realized that to add God to the end of a list doesn't solve the problem but just takes it back one stage further.

We don't need bad arguments like this one for God's existence. A false argument leads nowhere. And it can be no desire of a God of Truth that we use false arguments to persuade others—and perhaps ourselves of his existence.

Heavenly Father, help us to use our minds and our reason to discover more about you and your universe. And give us the courage to reject all false and misleading arguments. Amen.

Good Causes

Tony Hancock, in one of his television roles, once claimed that he was such a consistent supporter of 'flag days' that the lapels of his suits were always the first bits to go. It's a good thing to give as generously as you can to most appeals. They're usually in a good cause like Save the Children, Christian Aid, Oxfam or the National Association for Mental Health.

Of course, we haven't got an unlimited supply of money so we can't give to them all. We have to weigh up carefully which we think are the most important. Now most people wouldn't object at all to the societies and causes just mentioned. But there are sometimes subtle ways of moral blackmail—of making you feel guilty if you don't support a particular cause. And this moral blackmail should be resisted at all costs.

For example, in 1975 a national newspaper ran a campaign—not calling for money—but asking for the support through a petition of as many people as possible in their struggle against scientific experimenters who were using dogs to test the tar levels in cigarettes. The campaign was particularly slanted to appeal to children because the newspaper knew that young people have a great regard for animals and that schools are good places to pick up plenty of signatures. At that time many people, teachers and pupils alike, were made to feel in the wrong if they didn't support the newspaper's campaign. And yet the truth is that there are two sides to this issue of the smoking dogs.

First, there's the newspaper's point of view: that it's wrong to inflict disease on helpless animals in the interests of humans who can decide for themselves whether to smoke or not to smoke. Now that's a perfectly legitimate point of view, and if you agree with it then by all means sign the petition.

But secondly, there's the attitude which says human beings are more important than dogs. Cigarette smoking is dangerous to health. But some humans can't stop smoking. Therefore it's better to experiment on dogs in order to try and find a safer kind of of cigarette than to put human lives at risk. This is also a perfectly legitimate point of view. If you agree with this, then you ought not to sign the petition.

When faced with choices of this kind it is correct to refuse to be bullied and blackmailed into one opinion or the other, but to evaluate the cause as best you can and make your decision in the light of reason and conscience.

Heavenly Father, help us in the difficult task of making moral decisions. Amen.

The Good Old Days

We're always meeting folk who grumble about the present—now. They'll find anything to complain about, anything at all: motor bikes, long hair, tight trousers, flared trousers, football hooligans and even the weather. Maybe there's a lot wrong with the world, but perhaps grumbling on about it endlessly isn't the best way to solve our problems.

People who grumble about the present usually point to the past as a time when none of these bad things we're suffering existed. So they say, 'Ah it wasn't like that when I was a lad' and 'It was different in the good old days.' There's even a variety show called 'The Good Old Days' and it goes out from the City Varieties in Leeds.

Well, was it really so good? Was everything in the garden lovely in the time of our parents' and grandparents' childhood? A look at the history books and the newspapers of the day tells us that in many ways it certainly wasn't.

More women died in childbirth, more children in infancy. There wasn't a good health service then. People died of 'flu and measles. Men and women worked longer hours for much less money. Housing was worse. There was no old age pension. No paid holidays. And schoolteachers carried canes around with them. As for the weather—well you couldn't imagine better summers than those of 1975 and '76.

Of course, some things have deteriorated. Old people will tell you that folk were more friendly and neighbourly in the old days. And there weren't as many noises, smelly cars and lorries. The countryside wasn't as spoiled as it is nowadays.

But why is it that people always think that the past was better than the present, when obviously some things were better and others worse? Perhaps it's because we tend to forget the bad things and remember what pleases us. As if our minds act as blackboard rubbers which erase all unpleasant memories. Whatever the truth, our task remains to make the present time—today—as happy and as memorable as possible.

Heavenly Father, thankyou for happy memories. Help us to make good things in this present time. Amen.

Hang Up Your Boots

It's the newspapers' job to communicate as directly as possible with the public. They do it mainly through eye-catching headlines often of the 'Actress in Sex Spy Drama' variety. It all works on the principle that if you read the headline you'll read the article and if you read enough articles you'll buy the paper every day—or so the Editor hopes.

The use of headlines has made for the entrenchment of journalistic clichés and one of these clichés is the way the paper talks about people retiring. Footballers when they retire are said to 'hang up their boots'. Boxers 'hang up their gloves'. Stars on stage, screen and radio 'take their final bow'. Frequently it's not all that final either, because actors and actresses make many so called 'comebacks'.

The stage metaphor continues into politics. So if a statesman is defeated in an election it's 'Curtains for Heath' or 'Wilson Bows Out' and so on. It makes you wonder what they might say about retiring teachers. 'Hangs up his chalk'? 'Puts up the cane'? 'Closes the Book'? Teachers aren't really famous enough to attract such attention from the media, so they usually escape, and when they retire simply float off into oblivion.

All this shorthand, because that's what headline writing is a kind of shorthand, is very useful in getting a message across to a wide audience rapidly. But it's connected with another question altogether. Why are people identified with the jobs they do? You've all read the sort of story in the popular press where, for instance, coal miners have a night out at the ballet—or as happened some years ago, a titled lady was photographed playing a game of marbles in a cobbled street.

Well it's newsworthy of course—the unusual, the unexpected, the incongruous, the out-of-character activity. It wouldn't be of any interest to write about coal miners drinking in a working men's club or Lady So and So visiting the Chelsea Flower Show. No. Editors know that their readers want unusual and off beat stories of the 'man bites dog' variety.

It's just that sometimes in these interesting features, journalists seem to identify a person with the job he does. As if a cobbler cobbled all the time, or a teacher never left the classroom. And, of course, people are more than the way they earn their living. Men and women are all unique characters with individual lives. Behind every headline there's a human being.

Heavenly Father, help us not to judge others by first impressions or by reputation based on hearsay. Teach us to look for that unique quality which makes every person different from his neighbour. Amen.

I Only Want To Be With You

In the words of a popular song, 'It doesn't matter what you do; I only want to be with you.' It's an expression of love of course. When you love somebody the words of this song come true. Because you really don't care much about what they look like or about what other people might think of them. It's enough simply to be with them.

How different this is from all the reasons suggested to us in magazines why we should find people attractive and exciting. Sometimes we get the impression that it's absolutely necessary to use the right perfume, hairdressing, deodorant, toothpaste—even to favour one brand of soft margarine rather than another before anyone will love us. And this isn't true. We're loved and hated or simply ignored by different people because we've all got individual qualities and faults which attract some folks and repel others.

But even this is to use the word 'love' in a strange sense, because love isn't a matter of personalities at all but of loyalty and commitment; of care and concern; of putting someone else's good above our own.

It sounds a bit cold and clinical when it's put like that—like a sermon almost. But which is to be more greatly prized; to love someone, to care about him or her because we find him personally attractive, or to put someone else's well being above our own even when we don't find that person particularly attractive?

Long before Jesus, the wise man Lao Tse said that love should be returned for hate and good for evil. This might seem very hard, but Lao Tse says it's not the only proper thing to do, but it's also the most practical. And here's why. If someone insults you or does you some similar unkindness and you reply with the intention of revenge—of getting your own back—then a state of unease, war even, exists between the pair of you. But if you do good to those who hurt you, what then? Well, there's no opportunity for an argument or a feud to fester on and on. Love, in this sense, in unanswerable. It swallows up hatred because it doesn't allow the occasion for any further destructive mischief making. It is the most difficult, but, in the end, the only solution to problems which arise from our relationships with one another.

Heavenly Father, teach us to love even those whom we find the most unlovable. Help us to return good for evil and to do away with all opportunities for hatred. Amen.

In Whose Image?

The famous psychiatrist, Sigmund Freud, said that man created God and not, as the bible and religious teaching would have us believe, the other way round: God created man. Christians don't believe everything that Dr Freud said; in fact there aren't many people who do. But in a sense what he says about man creating God can be the source of constructive thought. Do people worship a God made in their own image?

Well, the gods of ancient Scandinavia—the Norse Gods—were Odin and Thor. Certainly their wild nature fits in with what we know of the history of the warlike Vikings. Such extremely powerful nature gods as these also seem to suit the rugged Scandinavian countryside.

And the Greek gods were generally lithe and beautiful young creatures not unlike the people who took part in the Olympic games of those days. Though sometimes some of them went a bit far with the merrymaking—again not unlike some of the ancient Greeks we read about.

Israel's God of the Old Testament was a spirit of mountain, wind and desert. Austere and uncompromising—just like a desert landscape in fact.

And the English have their God too. We can't be quite sure what he's like, but he's a gentleman of course. There's the story of the rather earnest young evangelical Christian who prayed each morning beginning: 'Lord, you will have read in *The Times* today . . . etc.' Certainly the quiet way in which we worship: orderly, precisely, in familiar oft-repeated words and seated in rows like peas in an English country garden, suggests that our God isn't given to rash or sudden behaviour. He likes to take life at a gentle, regular pace. These are all caricatures of course. God isn't made in man's image at all. He made man. But it would be foolish to deny that we all have local and national characteristics. So what could be more natural than that God, the true God, reveals aspects of himself through many different cultural traditions?

Heavenly Father, lead us from the worship of false gods, out of the hands of selfishness and the lust for power. Bring us ever more close to true knowledge of yourself. Amen.

It's Only Natural

You'll often hear people say of some activity or other, 'It's only natural'. Usually they say this as a kind of excuse when someone's done something wrong. For instance, parents might tell off their son or daughter for eating *all* the biscuits from the tin. But when the culprit's gone to bed, Mum might say, 'Well I suppose it was wrong of our Maggie, but after all it's only natural.' But you know this isn't really a good excuse at all.

Look at some of the other activities and events in the world which we call natural and you'll soon see that that in itself doesn't give us a reason for calling them good. Earthquakes are natural—but what suffering they cause! You could hardly call them good.

It's natural to kill and eat. But there are many aspects to that process which we don't readily applaud. And in human actions and creations we find good and bad mixed up together. It's natural, if you like, for a musician to compose music. Joseph Haydn composed a tune which was put to use as a hymn 'Praise the

Lord Ye Heavens Adore Him.' But the same tune was used by Adolf Hitler to rouse his bully boys to murderous fury.

The basic, raw, natural tune was put to one purpose that was good but to another that was evil. Nothing wrong with the music—the praise or the blame for its rightful or wrongful use lies with mankind.

Another thing that's perfectly natural is talking. We can give to one another a great deal of pleasure in conversation. But we can also use our voices to spread lies, curses and malicious gossip. Once again the basic activity—talking is quite natural. But that doesn't mean it's good. It's a neutral sort of thing. A raw material. What makes it good or bad is what we do with it.

And this is true about almost everything in the world. Very few things are good or bad in themselves. It's the way we operate with them which gives them their rightness or their wrongness. So next time you hear someone use the excuse, 'It's only natural' you might think of answering, 'Oh yes, I know it's natural, but is it good?'

Almighty Father, give us the will and the wisdom to use all things in the natural order for a good purpose. Amen.

It's the Same the Whole World Over

There was a poet called John Keats and here's something he wrote about a naughty boy:

There was a naughty boy,
And a naughty boy was he
He ran away to Scotland
The people for to see
Then he found that the ground was as hard
That a yard was as long
That a song was as merry
That a cherry was as red
That lead was as weighty
That fourscore was as eighty
That a door was as wooden as in England
So he stood in his shoes and he wondered.

Now John Keats isn't against travel. He's not saying 'Stay in the same place all your life and never move'. And as you may know Scotland of all places is very beautiful. There's the mountains, the rugged coastline and of course the lochs—perhaps one of them has a monster in it. And not Scotland alone—there are hundreds of places worth seeing and different things to do.

The point Keats is trying to get across to us is that basic things don't change just because of a shift in location. A yard is still three feet in Aberdeen. It's still three feet in Paris, and they have metres there. And you won't find maths any easier in Edinburgh than it is in London. As Keats says 'Fourscore (is) as eighty.'

More than all this the poet's really telling us that you and I are the same people wherever we go. Some folks think they can escape from their problems—escape in a way from themselves just by rushing off somewhere else. It's very tempting to imagine we can simply step out of our problems and difficulties in this fashion. But we can't.

One of the main tasks in growing up is to get to know ourselves—to learn to put up with ourselves, to face awkward and sometimes unpleasant facts about ourselves and our world just where we are now. Keats' boy in that poem wasn't really 'naughty', but he was rather silly to expect fundamental things to alter with the crossing of a national border.

Almighty God, help us to face our problems and to cope with our struggles however hard they seem to be. Amen.

Keys and White Coats

When you see someone walking around in a white coat you always thing that he's a person of some authority. He might be a doctor or a high-ranking engineer in a power station providing all our electricity. But he might just be an ordinary chap dressing up in a white coat for the fun of it—like people do in plays at the theatre. We still think of the white coat as a mark of authority of one kind or another. So we might say the white coat is a symbol. Symbols are visible objects which stand for invisible ideas.

There are as many symbols as there are ideas. Pieces of paper often symbolize the importance of a man's business. How often have you seen someone walking around with a bit of paper in his hand? He keeps staring at it, then in front of himself again—obviously on some extremely vital errand. But is he really? We can't be sure. But the bit of paper, the symbol, makes us think of importance.

Then there's motorbikes as symbols of power and energy. Flowers as symbols of life and tenderness. No doubt you can think of many others.

One of the most common of all symbols is the key or the bunch of keys. If you're sitting in a room with lots of other people, you can guarantee that, however many other folks are being ignored, if someone comes in jangling a bunch of keys, everyone will look up in curiosity and respect. Keys are symbols of power.

It's not hard to see why. After all, keys give us the power to control other people. If you've got a key, you can lock someone in or out. They're quite frightening objects really.

In the New Testament it says that Jesus gave Peter the keys of the kingdom of heaven. That's why we have all those pictures and jokes about Peter standing at the heavenly gates—giving and refusing different people entry into everlasting bliss.

It's all just a picture of course. There isn't really a man in the sky with a bunch of keys. But the fact that this picture has lasted so long is evidence of the power that symbols possess.

Think of half a dozen symbols before lunch.

Heavenly Father, thankyou for giving us signs and tokens by which we can understand your universe. Help us to understand the ideas of which symbols are the visible parts. Amen.

Language Goes on Holiday

When words don't seem to make sense you might say, 'Language has gone on holiday'. The philosopher, Ludwig Wittgenstein, talked about quaint and apparently meaningless uses of words as 'Language idling'.

So many examples of this turn up in what we read every day in the papers. Some words just don't mean what they look as if they should quite plainly mean. 'Re-building'. Ah, now there's a word to conjure with! How often places are closed for re-building. But one look inside tells you it doesn't seem to mean anything is actually being reconstructed. 'Rebuilding' often appears to mean quite the reverse—'knocking down'.

Then there's the estate agents' favourite—'compact' to advertise a house for sale. It doesn't mean 'compact' at all; it's a polite way of saying 'so small inside you couldn't swing a cat round.'

'Urban development' sounds good, doesn't it? It seems to mean 'flattening the centres of our cities and building multi-storey car parks instead'. And in political reports they say, 'A full and frank exchange of views' when they mean everybody had a row.

In a divided state people often refer to a 'Peace line'—but it means something vastly different. Usually an extremely dangerous border between the two warring factions.

You might like to try and think of a few examples of this kind of thing yourselves. Wittgenstein also said that the world we live in is very much a product of the language we use to describe it. By this he meant that words skilfully used can convey the very opposite effect of the real state of affairs but still create a picture that's believable. The estate agent's word 'compact' is a good example of this. It makes you think of neatness, tidiness, an uncluttered room—whereas in reality it means 'tiny'.

So we have a great responsibility in that when we use words we should be as accurate and as honest as possible. It's so easy to mislead by choosing the happy sounding word rather than the realistic one. A last thought: what do agricultural economists mean when they talk about 'the green pound'? Aren't *all* pounds green?

Heavenly Father, help us to use language honestly, accurately and creatively. Amen.

Little Boys and Girls

Honestly, some nursery rhymes should be reported to the sex discrimination people at the Equal Opportunities Commission! 'What are little girls made of? Sugar and spice and all that's nice—that's what little girls are made of!' And you know what's coming next, don't you? Quite right too. 'Slugs and snails and puppy dogs' tails—that's what little boys are made of!'

Really, such prejudice and bigotry you've never heard! And we'd be in a terrible state if it were true—which of course it isn't. But it's a myth that plays a very prominent part in the minds of some people. Girls? Ah yes, very nice creatures, long pretty hair and ribbons, smart and cheerful, softly spoken—though I'll bet you know a few who aren't! Yes, lovely people, girls—sweet, gentle and kind.

Now boys! They're awful—or so the myth would have us believe. Dirty, beastly, noisy and rude—always playing practical jokes and causing trouble. Well, of course it's not really true. Some boys are absolutely charming and just a few girls are—well perhaps it wouldn't be very gentlemanly to say exactly what they are.

But we shouldn't ban this little rhyme and begin a witch-hunt through all our fairy tales for material that says rude things about almost everybody. Such rhymes and tales as this one are quite colourful, sometimes make us laugh and usually do no harm. It would be a duller life without them.

But myths can be dangerous sometimes. Even jokes can be a menace if we take them too much to heart. Look at all the jokes about Irish people being stupid and all Jews and Scotsmen mean and stingy. The danger increases when we think of the more cruel jibes about all Italians being cowardly and all Germans as Nazis.

Of course, everybody should be able to take a joke—to laugh at himself; that's part of being fully human. But we should beware of the temptation to believe that because jokes amuse us they always tell us the truth. Often they don't. It's a good motto to remember that one thing you're not supposed to do with jokes is to take them seriously.

Heavenly Father, give us the ability to laugh at our own foolishness occasionally. Help us never to sneer at others. And deliver us from all prejudice. Amen.

A Little Learning

We've all heard stories of what schools were like in what some people called 'the good old days'. Pupils knew their place. None ever spoke unless spoken to by a master. Silence obtained at all times. And if anyone committed even the mildest misdemeanour, he faced execution—almost.

Now it's likely that schools never were quite so strict and orderly as some of the old times make out. But certainly the life of the traditional school song say of the 1920s and 1930s was much more formal than ours. The question arises, 'Did pupils learn more under the old regime than they learn under the new one?'

There is one idea about education that goes back much farther than the schooldays of our grandparents. T. L. Peacock in his *Nightmare Abbey* wrote:

> He was sent as usual to a public
> school where a little learning was
> painfully beaten into him. . . .

What an idea–that education and learning can be built on beatings and thrashings! It is true, of course, that schools were much stricter in the old days, but actually to suggest that learning can be beaten into a pupil is taking even the most traditional approach to schooling much further than anyone would now suggest.

And yet there's some truth behind what T. L. Peacock says. Not that the teacher should become over fond of the cane as a method of instruction, but that there's something about learning which we all find to be quite painful.

Educational psychologists and others whose business it is to discover how people learn have found out that when first introduced to a subject we learn quite quickly. But soon this progress slows down so that for quite long periods we can seem to be making no headway at all. This is the painful time. It's also the time to keep up our efforts, because although we might not appear to be advancing very quickly—if at all—the learning process is continuing. This is the time when work seems tedious and study painful. But if we want more than a *little* learning we must persevere during times of dullness and small reward.

Heavenly Father, help us when our studies seem hard and when books are long and heavy, to persevere in our task of learning. Amen.

The Longest Symphony in the World

I wonder if you think that science and art contradict each other. It does sometimes look as though they each offer rival explanations of the nature of the world. And it seems that if we accept one explanation we must reject the other. And yet we sometimes want to accept both.

I suppose a good example of this dilemma is the account of the world's creation in the Bible and the scientific version after Charles Darwin. You'll remember that Darwin said we all evolved very gradually over a period of millions of years. And the world was in existence for billions of years before that. But the Bible simply states that God made the world in seven days and put men and women on it straight away—instantaneous human beings in a garden.

The sound scientific training of the twentieth century obliges us to accept the rationality of Darwin's view. After all we can date rocks and fossils and make a fairly accurate time chart in order to guarantee the theory of evolution. But there's something about that Genesis story of Sun and Moon, night and day, man and woman—and the spirit of God moving over the face of the water that still appeals to us even when we know it to be a myth. It's as if scientists are people like those who tell us there's no Santa Claus—they may be right but they destroy the magic.

But I don't think there's reason for dismay here. Perhaps science and art, music or poetry are not rivals after all but partners. Maybe they all tell us something that's true but true in different ways. The botanist and the lover each offer us a different description of a rose, but we're not forced to reject the botany if we accept the poem.

A marvellous example of scientific doctrine and artistic creation going hand in hand can be seen in a piece of music by the composer, Gustav Mahler—in fact in his Third Symphony, the longest symphony in the world, over an hour and a half long. But it's not boring and hard to sit through in the concert hall. It's filled with tunes. And in his Third Symphony Mahler traces the evolution of the natural order from original chaos through the creation of rocks and flowers, the sun and animals, men, angels and finally the vision of God.

It's possible to listen to this great work and to see art and science not in conflict but in partnership.

In a moment's silence let us think of the splendour of the universe and man's talent for music, for science and art.

Lowry's Industrial Landscapes

Some people think that painting's all about quick flowing streams, autumn colours and rainbows. If you love the countryside and really appreciate time spent there, I suppose you might agree with them. Others think that pictures should shock and excite us by their outrageousness and originality. I'm sure you've seen so called modern paintings and wondered which way round the canvas should be.

There's one painter who didn't just produce beautiful country scenes and enticing pictures of beautiful ladies. And he didn't paint in what we've come to call 'modern art' either. His name was Lowry. Lowry's pictures are of life in the industrial towns of northern England in all their greyness and grime. But they're not dull and boring—far from it. There's something about them which is absolutely fascinating and I think it's the way Lowry paints his human figures.

From a distance these look like ordinary folk going about their daily work amid the chimneys and cobbled streets of Lancashire. But close up they don't look like people at all—but like blurred rectangles as if everyone was alike and no one had any particular individual existence or personality.

How frightening to imagine that people are not people at all but just shapes and blobs of dull colour. Of course it's not true. Everybody's an individual and a person in his own right. But I think one point Lowry's making is that our noisy, rushing, smokey, dirty, industrial society can make it look as though human beings are just blots on the landscape.

It's much cleaner in Lancashire now, but ordinary men and women still leave home every morning to spend a whole day in a world of machinery and mass-production. And it's the size and power of this technological machine which Lowry's paintings force us to recognize. It's so easy to feel small, dwarfed into insignificance even, by the gigantic structure of mechanization around us. Lowry's pictures help us to face this danger and to look again at ourselves as real people with individual personalities. Real people should never allow themselves to be made less than human by even the most enormous technological structure. People matter most.

Almighty God, help us to use our technological skill in order to make life not poorer but richer for all men and women. Amen.

Magic Numbers

I wonder if you're superstitious about numbers? Many people are you know. Won't go out of the house on the thirteenth of the month some of them—especially if it happens to be a Friday. Then there's the saying. 'Everything comes in threes', frequently spoken at a time of minor ill fortune in order to comfort the sufferer. So if you've fallen down the stairs on the way to breakfast, tripped over the cat while looking for your satchel and then slipped on a banana skin running for the school bus, a superstitious comforter might well say to you, 'Don't worry, everything comes in threes.' As much to say, after three pieces of ill luck your bad fortune's over. It's all right now.

Lots of numbers seem to carry magic significance. Seven is supposed to be lucky. All the years of a marriage are given a special meaning. Twenty-five years is a silver wedding, fifty a gold etc. . . .

Other numbers are odd in quite a different way. You know that the concept used in finding areas and circumferences of circles can be worked out forever in decimal places without coming to an end. And you can keep on halving any number for ever. You'll never get down to none. There's always a tiny bit left.

Because numbers are essential to calculations and plans for building everything from a garden shed to a moon rocket, it's not surprising we think of them as very important things. Pythagoras—you know the Greek who thought up the theorem about right-angle triangles—believed that the whole world was made out of numbers.

Now here's something to puzzle about. You would think that numbers can be divided into two groups—odd numbers and even numbers. And that the total of all the odd would equal the total of all the even. Quite right. But here's the puzzle: the total of even numbers *alone* is equal to the total of all numbers even and odd. Impossible? A contradiction? No, a fact because the number of numbers is infinite so the number of odd alone and even alone are also infinite. And since infinite = infinite then the total of even numbers alone is equal to the total of all numbers.

Almighty God, we thank you for the great mathematicians of the past and for our own ability to calculate and manipulate numbers to useful purpose. Amen.

The Magic Theatre

One thing about the theatre is that it makes everybody want to be an actor or an actress. You're sitting there in the middle of a ghost story or a comedy and you get that almost irresistible urge to join in. The other people in the hall might not like it if you did of course.

But imagine the theatre was real and that you could be in it doing anything you wanted to. There's a story about such a theatre. And in it there's a man who shoots motor cars and destroys them. That's what he likes doing most because he hates traffic so much.

Now, just think if only you could do anything you wanted to do in a magic theatre. You could create your heroes, friends or pop stars out of thin air. Imagine having Morecambe and Wise there in person and all to make you laugh—telling your favourite jokes even. And have just what you fancied to eat and drink. Great piles of ice cream and trifle. Gallons of coca cola and fresh orange juice. Your most exciting singers and dancers. And all for you.

Some people think that this would be the ideal life. All delight. Complete pleasure. No nasty tiresome work. No boring interruptions. No annoying teachers. A whole life of exactly what you want and nothing else getting in the way.

There's a bet though that such an existence, however attractive it seems at first sight, would turn out unsatisfactory before very long. People need a change. They need contrast. A little pleasure is good. A lot of pleasure is very good. But *all* pleasure would be a bore. And that's because part of any enjoyment is looking forward to it in the first place. And you couldn't do that if you were enjoying yourself all the time.

And it's also because human beings need challenge and work in order to be fully human. We all need to set ourselves tasks and struggles to test our strength and endurance. A programme on TV seems all the better if you've done a good day's work before you sit down to watch it.

Heavenly Father, help us in our work and in our leisure. Teach us to organize our lives so that we have suitable time for both. Amen.

Man Friday

For much of Daniel Defoe's novel, *Robinson Crusoe*, the hero is intensely lonely. Imagine being completely cut off, utterly alone on a desert island. It might seem a good thing for a time—at least in our imagination and wishful thinking—but hardly anyone could contemplate prolonged isolation and exclusion from his fellow beings.

So Defoe tells us how relieved Crusoe was to find that footprint in the sand and eventually meet Man Friday. A whole world was opened again for him in that day—conversation, the exchange of ideas, even just the sight of another human face.

From the time Crusoe met Friday there were two instead of one. Not what you'd call overcrowding, but far better than utter solitude. You can read *Robinson Crusoe* simply as a straightforward adventure story, but perhaps there's something else in it as well.

Some psychologists say that in every person there's two. The Self and the Shadow. Not a shadow like the one that's cast on the pavement in front of you by the sun. But another you—a dark side. A part of your nature that's very much you but isn't all that acceptable. Could it be that in a kind of pictorial way Man Friday is Robinson Crusoe's Shadow?

Well, whether he is or not, most of us would certainly admit that there's an aspect of our personalities that we don't like all that much. On a trivial level it's that bit of us that makes us want to grab the last piece of chocolate cake; to spend all our money on ourselves; to use other people for our own ends.

And this unacceptable part of us we can appropriately call the Shadow. Although it seems to be working for our interest, it's really working against us. You could grab the last bit of cake, but you'd feel rotten about it afterwards if you were to find out someone else had gone without altogether. And it's the Shadow that tells us to put off that important task in hand and to pursue some aimless activity instead. The Shadow encourages us to waste our time, to misunderstand and to misuse the world.

Maybe when Jesus met the Devil in the wilderness where he was tempted he was really meeting his shadow. That's perhaps what temptation is—a confrontation with the dark and destructive part of our own nature.

It's not that Man Friday was evil, just that in the mind of Daniel Defoe maybe the Shadow was so threatening that he had to find a pictorial and fictional role for it in one of his stories.

Almighty God, teach us to resist the demands of selfishness. Help us to consider the needs of others and to be patient. Amen.

The Man In The Moon On Sunday

When the Russians first went up into space they jibed 'We didn't find God up there.' And when Armstrong, Aldrin and Collins became the first men in the moon, they didn't claim to see the famous 'Man' who's supposed to be there. We've all heard of 'The Man in the Moon' and it's true that if you look at the moon's surface on a clear night you can make out what looks to be a face.

Of course we all know that the eyes, nose and mouth of the man in the moon are simply the shadows of lunar mountains and craters. But there's an old story about a man who was exiled or banished to the moon long, long ago.

It's only a legend, but you might ask 'What great crime did he commit in order to be transported all that way to solitary confinement?' And the answer is astonishingly that he was sent there for gathering sticks for firewood on Sunday.

That doesn't sound such a terrible offence but the story of the poor exiled man in the moon was told to generation after generation of children to stop them playing boisterous games on Sunday.

These days Sundays are very free and easy. Cinemas and dance halls are open. So are the pubs in most countries. But it wasn't always so. In the days of Queen Victoria, Sunday was a day of quiet and religious observance. Families went to church in the morning and spent the rest of the day reading the Bible or a suitable religious book like *Pilgrim's Progress*. There was certainly no playtime for children.

The odd thing about all this is that there's nothing specifically Christian about the dull Victorian Sabbath. In fact Christians don't keep Sunday as the Sabbath at all—Sabbaths are for Jewish people. Christians keep Sunday as a festival to remember the resurrection of Jesus and the Easter gift of new life. That seems to be something to rejoice about. To go to Church and maybe also to go to a dance. Certainly not to deserve exile to the moon.

Almighty God, help us to keep Sunday as a day of rejoicing for the gift of new life at Easter. Amen.

Micawber and The Family

Wilkins Micawber is a character in Charles Dickens' novel *David Copperfield* who's always waiting for 'something to turn up'. He means money usually because he's not very thrifty and tends to live in hope from one day to the next that a financial miracle will occur and keep him economically afloat.

The attitude of waiting for something to turn up can be destructive as well as frustrating. There's no harm in the occasional day dream of winning the football pools or being discovered by a long lost millionaire uncle. But when these activities take up so much of our time and imagination that they actually stop us getting on with the business of working life out for ourselves then they're a menace.

You could spend all your life dreaming that one day the England cricket selectors will call on your services to open the batting against Australia. You could day-dream through the motions of your maiden test century—in your first test naturally—at Lords. Or else you can idle the day away dreaming of either becoming a great pop star or marrying one. Carried to excess these activities are an utter waste of time.

But there is a reasonable way of hoping for the best. It's fair enough to hope for a fine day for the school sports, or that your team will win an important game. And it's reasonable to hope that fair effort on your part might be fairly rewarded.

There's even another kind of hope that Wilkins Micawber never even thought of. You could call it 'the cavalry come riding over the hill'. We've all seen those westerns where everyone's surrounded by bloodthirsty renegade Indians, utterly defenceless and about to be scalped. Suddenly there's a bugle. The cavalry comes over the hill and all's well.

This kind of hope is that ultimately, no matter how desperate the situation is, God will not let us down. He won't allow us to suffer more than we can bear. And, although justice may not always be seen to be done in this world, there is more to God's plan for us than this world can contain.

Heavenly Father, help us to hope realistically and not to waste our lives in fond speculation. Give us the sure hope that, however bad things get, you are always with us. Amen.

Midwinter Spring

From November till February the weather's nearly always gloomy. The pavement never dries out properly and it always looks dirty. Clouds overhang buildings in the distance and you can't see very far. It's cold of course. Grey. Drab. Miserable. Damp. Nothing to look forward to. It's enough to make anyone feel depressed. You can't remember the summer, it seems so long ago. And spring is simply ages away.

As if this weren't enough, your feet get cold and you start sneezing. What a miserable time of year. Then suddenly, perhaps in early January, you wake up to a day that's utterly different. There's not a cloud in the sky. The sun is bright as in a July heat wave. It's drying the last bits of melted frost from the roofs of town houses.

Perhaps there's a coating of frost on the black twigs on the small bushes. But even this could be mistaken for blossom. What a marvellous day! We don't get many like this, but in the worst winter months there are usually one or two. People cheer up. 'It's like spring' they say. But of course it's not spring. There's much of winter yet to come. And the air is still cold. Not the day to go out without a sweater.

In 'Little Gidding', one of T. S. Eliot's *Four Quartets*, the poet wonderfully describes such a day as 'Midwinter Spring'—wonderful because that's just what it is. A spring day out of season. Except Eliot goes on to say it's not out of season. 'Midwinter spring is its own season' he writes. He thinks of such a day as a magical time of year, and in 'Little Gidding' he captures the flavour of midwinter spring exactly.

Eliot goes on: 'Sempiternal though sodden before sundown'. We know just what he means. Our magical midwinter spring looks as if it could last forever but we know that even before the sunset, the pavements will turn damp again and perhaps the mist will close in.

Undoubtedly there's sadness in our midwinter spring simply because we know it can't last. But we should also be comforted by it as a reminder that the real spring will follow winter–and that's a promise.

Almighty God, thankyou for glorious winter days, for midwinter spring. Give us strength and patience in the dark days in winter. Amen.

More Than Coincidence

They say truth's stranger than fiction. Well there are lots of events that puzzle us and none more so than coincidences. If you meet your best friend quite accidently at, say, the Youth Club or the match on Saturday that's not much of a coincidence, especially if he often goes to the same club as you or if he's a keen football supporter.

But there are much more weird coincidences than these. Suppose you're sitting in the library reading about natural history. And suppose you come across the word 'butterfly'. At that very moment two girls walk past where you're sitting and one whispers to the other. 'Oh, she can't settle down to any job. She's a proper *butterfly*.'

Now butterfly is a word which everyone understands, but it's not used so frequently that you'd expect it to be spoken by two sets of quite different people in different conversations at the same time. So what kind of event is this?

A thinker named Carl Jung named such events as instances of what he regarded as 'synchronicity'—oddly similar events happening at the same time.

The strange thing about these events is that they can't be explained by cause and effect. The girls' mention of the butterfly didn't cause you to read the word 'butterfly.' No. It seems as if quite a different kind of principle from cause and effect is at work here.

But as Carl Jung pointed out, he wasn't the first to notice synchronicity—he didn't invent it. He only thought of the word. Ancient people were great believers in the odd association of peculiarly similar events. So, for instance, it's said that a comet appeared in the sky to mark the birth of Julius Caesar. That there was an eclipse of the sun at the time of the crucifixion.

Scientists are beginning to investigate synchronicity. Why do such odd coincidences happen? If they happen according to some kind of principle then that could be very useful knowledge not just for the scientists but for us all.

Almighty God, we thank you for curiosity and enquiring minds. Help us to use our intelligence creatively so that we may understand the world in fresh ways. Amen.

Mozart's Summer Holiday

I don't know what you're going to do in the holidays. Of course, I hope you'll have a good time and that you won't come to any harm—drown in the sea or fall down a pothole or anything awful like that.

But whatever we do in the holidays we think of them as a time for rest, for recharging the batteries. Even teachers get tired of school towards the end of term you know. And if you're not going away anywhere special you can still have a good time near home. There's nothing like just idling about for a week or so.

But it gets a bit boring—just idling about I mean—after about ten days or a fortnight. I think the composer Wolfgang Mozart must have found out something like that because when he was nineteen, in the summer of 1776, when he could have been taking life a bit easier, he wrote five violin concertos. He'd never written a violin concerto before, and as I said he was only nineteen, but incredibly he wrote five in only a very few weeks.

I don't suppose you'll all take to writing symphonies and dictionaries this summer, but I'll make an honest bet with you. And that's that after a few days of idling and messing about, you'll find the holiday a lot more interesting if you take up some sort of pastime like walking, or playing some regular sport, or fishing—but mind you don't fall in—or anything really. It doesn't matter what you do as long as it's something you apply yourself to on a regular basis. And you'll come back, even to school, feeling as if you've had a holiday.

Heavenly Father, thankyou for the excitement of the end of term. Bless our holiday. And help us to recreate and refresh ourselves in mind and body during the summer weeks. If we get bored help us to find interesting and enjoyable things to do. Amen.

Music Time

If you were trying to judge an age—to make some comment about a period of history—to sum up how people lived in particular time, what would you choose? Not just 'what were the principal industries' kind of description, but a summary that tries to capture the flavour of an age?' What did it feel like to be, say, an English subject in the eighteenth century?

You could choose costume and clothes. People in the eighteenth century, for instance, went in for elaborate dress. Wigs and bright tunics for men; large colourful dresses for ladies. Then there were the original Teddy Boys in the early part of our own century. Drainpipe trousers, thick-soled shoes and very lengthy velvet jackets. And there's been a long period when men have dressed in a particularly drab sort of way. Grey suits. White shirts. Sober ties and sensible shoes.

Or you could choose architecture instead. Frequently the buildings men erect tell us a lot about the men who built them. How the concise, logical, geometrical precision of Corinthian columns and triangular arches reflect the thoughtful, mathematical, disciplined and philosophical nature of the ancient Greeks.

And the higgledy-piggledy mixture that was Victorian architecture fits in well with that age which borrowed ideas in bits and pieces from all previous ones. So to the present. What do our square, characterless constructions have to say about us? Are we really as dull and square as our buildings? It's much more difficult to judge a period you're actually living through than one that's long past. New events occur so our assessment is always changing.

Perhaps we're not so dull and boring after all. Maybe we've returned to simple shapes in order to start building exotically once again—perhaps in a few years time. The German writer, Wolfgang Goethe, once said that architecture was like frozen music. He meant music preserved in stone would probably look like architecture. It's certainly a very poetic statement.

So what might our modern music say about the age we live in? It might appear that both popular and so called 'serious' music has returned to a basic simple structure—pausing for self-examination almost before something more adventurous is created.

Certainly we live in very uncertain times—with the bomb, the problems about population, world resources and terrorism. Maybe music and architecture represent our modern age in two quite different ways. Music, jangly, discordant and often unpredictable, captures the uncertainty of our time. And in the face of this perplexity we construct good, solid, square structures as a kind of symbolic comfort and assurance.

Heavenly Father, thankyou for created beauty. For art and architecture, music and dance. Amen.

No News is Good News

I suppose you've heard the expression 'No news is good news.' It's usually uttered when someone, perhaps belonging to the family, hasn't been heard of for some time. So, quelling their anxiety with a large dose of optimism, people comfort themselves with the thought that no news is truly a sign of good news.

But when you watch the news on television or read the papers it really does look as if no news is good news—in quite a *different* sense though. It looks as if all news is bad news. Earthquakes, wars, epidemics, bridges collapsing, aircraft crashing, ships sinking, crops ruined, roads blocked, people starving, politicians lying, people cheating etc. . . . etc. . . . You could go on forever about bad news.

I wonder why it's only the bad news that gets reported? In its early days you know, the BBC used to cancel its news broadcasts if it couldn't find anything to report. The reader used to come on and say 'There's no news tonight.' Well, fancy that! There must have been news! The world doesn't stop just because nothing particularly noteworthy has come to the attention of BBC journalists. I expect what they really meant when they said 'There is no news tonight' was that no wars had broken out, no particularly nasty accidents had occurred and England had managed not yet to have lost the test match.

Fair enough really, I suppose. But I can't help thinking why didn't they come on in the absence of calamities and give us some good news? What a golden opportunity to tell us it's been sunny all day in Wales, or that the 9.23 at Waterloo was on time, that nobody was sent off in the day's football games.

The fact is, of course, that it's bad news that sells papers. We don't really like good news. It bores us. Just imagine a newsreader saying something like 'There were no crashes on the M1 today. The world is at peace. All statesmen agree about everything. And the weather is absolutely ideal.' We'd be bored silly by this kind of thing. What turns our attention to the television news is pictures of overturned trains, air crashes and natural disasters.

But I don't think this is because we want these bad things to happen. I think there's grounds for hope in the fact that mostly only bad news gets reported. Perhaps, because good news seems boring, it means that good news is more common than bad. And maybe the reason people turn to their televisions when natural disasters and traffic accidents are shown is that they care about what's happening to their fellow human beings.

Heavenly Father, we pray for all those whose business it is to report the news—for those who work in television and on newspapers. And we ask your blessing on all who have recently suffered through accidents and natural disasters.

Oedipus and the Sphinx

In the poem 'Don Juan' by Byron are the lines:

> But I'm not Oedipus and Life's a Sphinx;
> I tell the tale as it was told, nor dare
> to venture a solution.

Oedipus was the only person to be able to answer the Sphinx's riddle. And Byron is here telling us that life is ultimately a mystery. It is a task to be lived not a conundrum in need of solution.

It is of course true that from time to time we all wonder why we're here and what the universe is for. There seem to be so many conflicting answers and contradictions. For instance, if God is all-powerful and completely good, then why does he permit suffering?

And sometimes the weight of such questions as this bears down upon us, bears down upon us with such force that we try to forget about them and seek a hiding place or an escape into rather ignoble pursuits. Many a man has turned in doubt and desperation to drink, to opium or the pursuit of wild adventure. And all because life presents itself as a riddle of the sphinx; a question which we can't answer, but at the same time can't avoid.

Philosophers and theologians throughout our history have struggled towards tentative answers to the problems of human existence and whether life has a purpose and meaning or not. And no sooner is a tentative answer found than it proves to be only a stop gap, an incomplete solution and in the end just another way of squaring up to the original problem.

So perhaps the best course isn't endless speculation—sharpening and occasionally illuminating and pleasurable though that may be—but commitment to someone in faith. To live life as if it has meaning and then perhaps we'll find that it has. For as Byron says: 'But I'm not Oedipus and Life's a Sphinx.' It could be that in this section from 'Don Juan' the poet speaks for us all.

Heavenly Father, give us more faith and more trust. Help us to live our lives with courage in the face of unanswerable questions and do not leave us without hope. Amen.

The Old Man of the Tribe

Here is part of a schoolteacher's recollection of his time as a boy in a Northern town.

'Near where I used to live when I was a boy was a park. And on this park near the swings and roundabouts was an old man's shelter. Every afternoon, even when it was raining, retired railway signalmen and bus drivers, men who'd spent a lifetime clocking in regularly at mills and factories, used to wander out to this round shelter with windows of dirty glass. And there they used to play dominoes. I think they played for money, only small stakes though, because you don't have a lot of cash if you're an old age pensioner. I used to meet one old chap—he always wore the same dark grey overcoat whatever the weather—and I used to get into conversation with him as he was on his way home for tea.

'He'd been a packer in a nearby warehouse for forty-three years and now he was retired. I called him Uncle Joe. And he told me about a thousand and one different things. How the world war had started, what it was like to live in Leeds during the slump and how in the last war he'd been a part-time fire watcher with his mates—in a sort of Dad's army. One thing he kept telling me was how much better, how much easier it was nowadays than it had been when he was a lad. People had more money now and were better fed and looked after. And yet I couldn't help getting the idea that he thought that somehow the old days were better. People were poorer but there was more sense of belonging, of what we might call community. Now I'm not saying that all the improvements in medical care, diet and provision in smart new senior citizens' homes are a bad thing—they're not. But sometimes I think that by packing off our old folk to an old people's home—however plush and modern—everybody loses something of great value. In some societies old people live in the family home and they're respected for their wisdom. Grandpa becomes the wise old man of the tribe.'

Perhaps we should remember that however full of energy and the latest ideas we might think ourselves to be and how ever much we grow impatient with some of the slowness of old aged people they can give us something which as young or youngish people we don't have: I mean the benefit of experience and a highly personal and fascinating account of how things were for our locality in what some children call 'the olden days'.

Get to know an old person near your home. Call in to see if she needs you to run any errands. I'll bet you'll be made welcome. And I'll guarantee you won't be bored.

Heavenly Father, thankyou for the liveliness and enthusiasm of youth and for the wisdom and experience of old age. Help us to be sensitive to the needs of old people. Amen.

The Onion Bag and the Tu-Tu

One night watching a ballet called 'Coppélia' by Delibes on television a five-year-old boy asked his eight-year-old sister: 'What do they make those dresses called tu-tus out of?' 'It's a sort of nylon or net I think,' replied the eight year old knowledgeably, 'a bit like the bag that your mother gets the onions in.'

It's true of course. But fancy that. Fancy comparing an exquisitely delicate ballet dress with an onion bag. It sounds all wrong; inappropriate, rude, philistine. But it's not all that silly really. Ballet dresses and onion bags are both made out of net—and net's net all the world over, however fine, however coarse. It's one substance.

And this leads to something quite interesting. Some ancient people believed that everything—not just tu-tus and onion bags—but absolutely everything was in the first place made out of one substance. They thought that the world began with some sort of primeval stuff so that all the different substances as we know and call them really boil down to the same thing in the end. Perhaps modern chemists and physicists might want to find fault with this point of view. But even if it's not strictly true, there's a meaning in this idea that the ancients had—a meaning that can be a kind of parable for us. It gives us a strange sense of belonging. An 'all in the same boat' feeling.

And in a way it's true in a quite straightforward way. We really do share the nature of everything else in the universe. We grow. We change. We die. Perhaps we even enter a new life at that moment of what we call 'death'. Like the caterpillar and the butterfly? Who can tell?

But more than this, perhaps most importantly, we're all depending on one another all the time in the same way we depend on materials. Just as we need the wood in the desk top to remain firm so that we can rest our notebooks on it, so we need our friends to remain constant and faithful to us in a personal sense. In our world everyone depends upon everyone else.

Heavenly Father, help us to realize how much we depend upon one another and give us courage and strength so that we can trust and be trusted. Amen.

Pagan?

People think of lots of names to insult you with. It's most upsetting to be called a nuisance. That's somebody who's of no use but always in the way. Like pest. Makes you feel as if you're a wasp or a bluebottle. Something unpleasant like that.

Then there's 'stupid'. Nobody likes to be thought stupid. Empty headed. No brains. Along with this go the equally unpleasant 'idiot' 'dolt', 'nincompoop' etc.

And there are all those vices which no one wants us to have. 'Nosey-Parker': someone who's always poking his nose into other people's business. 'Big head': pompous conceited person. 'Know-All': that means roughly the same. And 'gas bag': an expression to describe someone who makes a lot of noise without saying anything interesting or important.

One description that's almost an insult is 'pagan'. It carries with it the idea that the pagan is without belief, without civilization, without humanity almost. And yet if we look at the origin of this word, we can see that it didn't always carry such an offensive meaning.

'Pagan' used to mean 'of the local place' or 'belonging to the village'. And it just stood for those customs and activities which belonged specially to a particular location. So pagan customs were originally local customs.

'Pagan' became a dirty word when the nation state gained supremacy over the self-governing local province. And it happened in religion too. As soon as Christianity became established as a national and even an international religion—the small town gods and the small town customs were outlawed. In a way it was bound to happen in order to secure a unified state.

But in one respect it was a bad thing. National and international traditions, while very good in themselves, encouraged folk to forget their own local customs and the individual special contributions that the small independent community can make. Not that we should all become pagans again—just that we might gain a lot of information and enjoyment out of discovering what's special to our own local community.

Heavenly Father, thankyou for our traditions. Help us never to reject an idea simply because it has become associated with an unpopular word. But give us wisdom to learn all the good lessons of history. Amen.

Pale Galilean—Was Jesus A Colourless Character?

What astonishing ideas people sometimes get about characters from history. In particular there are some very odd notions knocking about which concern Jesus. Whether you believe that he was the Son of God or whatever is a matter for your own decision. But whoever Jesus was, he certainly wasn't dull or boring.

And yet Algernon Charles Swinburne, writing in the last century says of Jesus: 'You have conquered O Pale Galilean, and the world has grown grey from your breath.' Pale Galilean? Grown grey? What a weak and ineffective person Swinburne suggests Jesus was. But on what evidence?

It couldn't be on the account of the call of the disciples. Does Mr Swinburne really think that burly, tough and weather hardened fishermen would, at a minute's notice, up and follow a weak and insipid character?

And what about that incident where Jesus charges into the court of the temple and drives out the dealers in pigeons with a whip? He must have been a strong man to do that.

There are countless examples of a lively, courageous and attractive Jesus which really do make it look as if Swinburne was talking nonsense. There's the courage of Jesus before Pilate; his bravery at the time of his execution; the way he stood up to the corrupt religious authorities of the time—even though they had the power to have him crucified. In fact the gospels present a Jesus who is anything but weak—a Jesus who's certainly not a pale copy of a human being.

But, you know, it's rare for anybody ever to be either completely wrong or completely right. Maybe there's something in what Swinburne says (not about Jesus) but about his followers—the church.

Perhaps sometimes you wonder how such a dynamic character as Jesus certainly was could give rise to some of the most quiet and faint-hearted folk you could wish to avoid.

If you go to a church service you're likely to meet a lot of rather long faces and to be confronted with the spectacle of people taking themselves very seriously indeed. Many church people seem to be like this. They appear to be against all forms of pleasure and any hint that you can be a Christian and enjoy life.

Well, it's not supposed to be like that. Jesus generated a faith full of life and joy. But churchpeople should realize that their founder will be judged through them. And if they radiate dullness then people like Swinburne will continue to find their founder 'pale'.

Heavenly Father, help us especially when we feel miserable, not to give in to disappointment and dejection. Help us to be courageous. Help us to be joyful. Amen.

Pasali and Treacle

If you like treacle you'd like the Hindu Festival of Pasali Day because then young Hindus meet together to share a special dish of butter and treacle. It happens every year in the summer on a Sunday round about the end of July or the beginning of August.

Pasali comes at a time which is most sacred to Hindus. In a way it's a bit like the Christian season of Lent. In the Christian church it's a custom not to get married until Lent is over and the joyful season of Easter has arrived. So the days around Pasali are regarded in a similar way and not many Indians marry at that time of the year.

Maybe it seems odd that great faiths like Hinduism and Christianity, which teach that men and women are loved by God, should have seasons of sadness and gloom. If you go into an English church during Lent you're likely to find no flowers there and the building stripped of many of its usual bright decorations. Even statues and crosses are sometimes covered with plain cloth.

And in the days around Pasali Hindus pay special worship to Shiva the destroyer. Left like that it could all sound very miserable indeed. But when we think of Lent we also look forward to the Easter triumph which follows after. Of the spring flowers and warm sunshine which come after the winter's gloom. It is as if the church calendar follows the natural seasons of the year.

And it's the same with the sacred season around Pasali. At the end of these quiet and sacred days there follows the celebration of the birthday of one of the most popular of all Hindu gods—Krishna.

What do both Christianity and Hinduism teach here? That a triumph follows only after the proper prayer and reflexion about the year just past. But Pasali is sweetened by treacle as Lent is by pancakes on Shrove Tuesday.

Heavenly Father, when sadness comes help us to bear it. And teach us to use sorrowful times to look inward and examine our hearts and minds. Amen.

Pickles' Embarrassing Moment

Long ago on the old steam radio a man called Wilfred Pickles and his wife, Mabel, used to run a programme called 'Have a Go'. It was nearly always presented from a local village or church hall, and it always attracted a large audience both live and on the wireless.

Members of the public were invited up onto the stage where they were interviewed by Wilfred. It was all very light hearted. They'd say a few things about themselves and answer a simple question or two and take away a couple of pounds for the privilege when Pickles said, 'Give him the money, Mabel!'

Wilfred Pickles didn't ask hard questions but he did come up with some interesting ones—and his guests often gave some even more interesting answers. The question that always provoked the most giggles was, 'Have you ever had an embarassing experience?' Well you can imagine the sorts of replies. People caught with trousers down or finding themselves without cash after eating a big meal in a restaurant. You could imagine the candidates' blushes. You had to because there was no television in those days. It's a funny thing how radio is sometimes even better than television. What we imagine is often more real than what we see.

Anyhow, this business about feeling embarrassed. Why was it such a success on 'Have a Go'? Why was the embarrassing moment everybody's favourite part of the show?

Perhaps it's because we've all been embarrassed at one time or another and so we can understand what Wilfred's guests were feeling. We can identify with them.

On the television Jonathan Miller once told what happens when someone trips up in the street. He regains his balance as quickly as possible, and then in an over acted way he turns round and points and stares accusingly at the crack in the pavement. It's as if he's saying, 'It wasn't my fault; it was that crack.' And he does this because he's embarrassed.

Embarrassment is a marvellous thing—a gift from God even—although you may not think so. You see all the time, or nearly all the time, we pretend we're so very dignified and in control. Then suddenly we slip on a banana skin and lose our balance and our poise. The result is everybody laughs. Even we laugh eventually. Pickles' show and Miller's explanation interest us all because they tell us something about ourselves. You might say that being embarrassed is being caught out being human.

Heavenly Father, thankyou for laughter and for comedians and clowns who entertain us. Help us to be able to laugh at ourselves sometimes. Amen.

The Picture and the Diagram

It's absolutely amazing that the police ever catch any criminals at all if they're guided by those photofit pictures. They just don't look like anybody at all. And of course that means they could be pictures of anybody. But that's just it. They're not pictures at all really. They're diagrams.

The lady novelist, Marian Evans, or George Eliot as she liked to be known, once wrote to a friend the following words, 'I have no wish to lapse from the picture to the diagram.' George Eliot's friend was asking her to put her name to something which the great novelist thought to be artificial, pretentious and contrived. Something less than real. Something more like a diagram than a picture.

Now it's not that diagrams aren't useful. Sometimes they're absolutely necessary—especially if you're not a very practical person and you're trying to wire a plug or something like that. Countryside and street maps are kinds of diagrams—extremely useful kinds of diagrams which enable us to find our destinations instead of getting lost.

But diagrams are dangerous if we take the information they give us too literally. Of course nobody would mistake a photofit of a face for a photograph. But people often make a similar error. We're apt to imagine we can sum someone up or account for him by a verbal diagram. You know the kind of thing, shorthand descriptions like 'The tall thin one', 'The little fat one' and so on.

In fact men and women, boys and girls are infinitely more complex than any diagram; far more complicated than the glib phrases we occasionally use to refer to one another suggest.

Shorthand and diagrams have their uses. The police do catch criminals from photofits. But George Eliot's words, 'I have no wish to lapse from the picture to the diagram', should remind us that human beings are individual works of art and not merely successful technology.

Almighty Father, help us to look at one another with respect. Teach us never to treat our neighbours as if they were puppets or machines. Amen.

The Pit and the Pendulum

There's a horror film with Vincent Price in it called 'The Pit and the Pendulum'—perhaps you've seen it. It's enough to give anybody the shivers. It's about a terrible torture chamber in a dungeon. Vincent Price plays the villian and he's got some frightening contraptions and instruments of terror in his spooky cellar. The worst is a giant blade suspended from the ceiling by a cord which causes the blade to swing like a pendulum. And everything is so horribly arranged that, with every swing, the sword swings closer to the hero's exposed chest. He's tied up lying on a stone slab exactly beneath this evil machinery.

No doubt you know the story. Rescue comes just in time and the hero escapes. But Vincent Price gets his just reward for all his evil tricks. It's a very, very scary film, and if you're the sort who has nightmares don't watch it next time it comes on the television.

I wonder why most of us delight so much in horror films? Millions of people do, you know, or else the picture makers wouldn't keep making them and making a lot of money for themselves in the process. There's 'Dracula' and 'Frankenstein', 'Werewolves' and 'Gorgons'. Some folks watch every one. Why do we like being scared almost to death?

Perhaps it's got something to do with a kind of false courage. I mean it's all right, it's safe to lock the front door, put the little reading lamp on and curl up on the settee to enjoy being frightened because it's not real, is it? No matter how scared you get; no matter how much you imagine that it's you on that table under the crunching blade and Vincent Price's evil grin, it's not true. You're safe in your own home eating peanuts and drinking lemonade. But you can imagine that you're really the hero undergoing the most awful tests in the cause of justice and right. There's usually a pretty girl for the hero too.

And all that's why horror films are, perhaps, good for us after all. Because they allow us to feel the sensation, the emotion of fear without actually being in any real danger. For a lot of the time our lives are concerned with routine, so a bit of fantasy in the form of a western, a musical or even a horror film with Mr Price in it offers us a little dream—an alternative life for an hour or so. A rest from the strain of being ourselves.

Heavenly Father, thankyou for entertainment. For plays and films and for those who take part in them. We ask your blessing on those who work in the —— Theatre in our town. Amen.

Poison Gas

Sometimes when you get home from school—especially on a Monday I think—you don't feel like doing much work. I mean Monday's first day back after the weekend and by the time you've dragged yourself through the day it seems enough to settle down in the evening after a meal and maybe read a book or see if there's anything good on the television.

Not so long ago I was watching the TV one Monday evening when one of these pretty scary science fiction films came on. It was all about poison gas. It's proper name was 'nerve gas', I think. Anyway it was all about an evil genius—a sort of a mad scientist with an evil grin—and he'd invented a terrible poison. And he was holding the United Nations to ransom with it. Perhaps you saw the film? Anyway you know the kind of thing I mean. Dr Morbius, or whatever the evil scientist was called, was threatening to poison the world unless he was given lots of money and power.

And the poison gas was horrible stuff. It worked by paralysing everybody who came into contact with it. And it was spread by human contact. The evil Morbius dropped a tiny globule of his nerve gas in order to demonstrate his power. But the trouble was once the poison had started to spread there was no way of stopping it. People were dropping like flies. Eventually, the hero and his girl friend found an antidote of course and everybody was made well again and Morbius thrown into prison. It was a good film with lots of action in it.

When it was over I started thinking about the way Morbius' nerve gas was spread. It was handed on by human contact. And the antidote was communicated in the same way. That's what it's like really in school, in the world isn't it? Not with nerve gas of course but with good and bad. If people become angry and jealous and bitter then a kind of evil atmosphere spreads. But if folks are good humoured, kind of considerate of one another's needs, then there's a happy and pleasant spirit about the place.

Almighty God, teach us that we are responsible for one another's happiness. Help us in our attitudes towards everybody we meet to spread a caring generous spirit. Amen.

Popular Music

Some people are very snobbish when it comes to music. They like to go to symphony concerts and organ recitals and then talk as if they've done something which somehow makes them better than anyone else. Of course, there's nothing wrong with going to concerts—it's the snobbish attitude that's the fault.

If you don't like Beethoven and Chopin and Brahms all that much but prefer the sort of music you get on 'Top of the Pops', the music snobs look down on you and sneer. They like doing this because it makes them feel superior. They say that 'classical' music is what you listen to and that the pop stuff is just a load of old rubbish.

You know that this isn't true. Some pop music is poor; it's dull and monotonous. While other popular songs and tunes are marvellous, catchy and carry a strong atmosphere and meaning with them. Well, some frequently played so-called 'classical' music isn't all that good either. There's wonderful Mozart and rather more mediocre Mozart. Goodness isn't a quality shared by only one kind of thing. There are good and bad examples of all kinds of art—and that goes for music from any period whether it's eighteenth-century or the late 70s.

Now there's a strange thing that musical snobs are frequently keen to tell us—that's how many of the great composers were neglected and ignored by audiences in their day, and how many of them even starved to death. It's quite true, Schubert died when he was thirty-one—he caught a cold at Beethoven's funeral. Mozart died at thirty-five. And there are many more examples. The music snobs, in telling us this, are trying to imply that if only they'd been around in those days they wouldn't have let the master musicians starve to death. They would have appreciated their music.

Well, how do we know they would? It would be good if there were a way of testing this. And happily there is. You see there are people about today writing what might loosely be called 'serious' or 'classical' music. So how do the music snobs react to them? They ignore their concerts. They criticize their work without attempting to understand it. And if, as a result of neglect, some modern composers are driven to give up music, who will the musical snobs of the twenty-first century blame then?

Of course many lovers of classical music are much more open minded than this and love music for its own sake and not for any prestige which they think comes through being the kind of person who goes to concerts. But beware of the snobs, pity them and don't become like them. You'll end up missing so much.

Heavenly Father, help us appreciate the music and art of all ages. Amen.

Psapho's Birds and the Ad-men

It's amazing what people will believe. They'll even believe that men are gods if they're told to. Once there was a character called Psapho who thought a lot of himself. Praise-hungry chap that he was, he decided to teach some talking birds to repeat 'Psapho's a God' so that those who heard it would be inclined to worship him.

And, so the story goes, a whole continent came to think of Psapho as a god just because of the birds repetitious phrase, 'Psapho's a god'. What good this finally did Psapho isn't at all clear.

But we're not like those poor fools who believed the talking birds are we? We wouldn't believe just anything we're told. Perhaps primitive people would take notice of apparently magical birds—but not us. Not us today with our critical minds and our ability to spot when we're taken for a ride.

Something else seems to have taken the place of Psapho's birds in our own time. And we really do sit up and take notice of it. That's the television. We like to think we're not influenced by the adverts and some of the programmes to spend our money on what we don't really want to spend it. But we delude ourselves. And we are taken in by the box and by other forms of advertising.

Look how many bionic tee-shirts and action dolls the Steve Austin craze sold. Think of the number of records that are bought after they've first been heard on 'Top of the Pops'. Notice which cat food your parents buy—and ask them what made them choose that particular one. Everything from clothes to continental quilts, toys to toothpaste are whispered, sung or shouted at us in the same seductive tones as Psapho's birds sang that their trainer was a god. It's good to have the opportunity to choose between one product and another. That's one of the benefits of advertising. But it's even better to be able to resist even the most persuasive suggestion that we buy something we don't really want.

Heavenly Father, help us to be sensible and discerning in the way we spend our money. Teach us to appreciate things for their real value and not simply as passing fancies. Amen.

Pure Gold

They've been exploring Stonehenge, which looks like a ring of great croquet hoops in the South of England. Nobody has ever been able to come up with an entirely satisfactory explanation for this weird arrangement of rocks out on the moor. Some say it was a religious shrine used by those ancient priests, the Druids. But recently some scientists have been claiming that primitive people were not half so primitive as we might think them to be. They're saying that Stonehenge was a pre-historic observatory.

Now what would iron-age folk want with an observatory? They had no telescopes, no rockets, no space exploration. How could the stars and planets, the sun and moon be of possible interest for them? Well, apparently we're finding out that the ancients in Britain were good at maths and keen on calculations and equations. Even that they could predict the patterns of stars in the night sky and the eclipses of the moon and sun.

If you're living a primitive life without electricity and central heating as they were, then it becomes pretty important to be able to calculate eclipses and the onset of the cold dark winter. So the sun which the ancient Britons observed from Stonehenge was of vital concern for them. It was their life, light and warmth; the plain and obvious source of all their existence.

And the colour of the sun is of course yellow or golden. Perhaps this is why even today we regard gold as something precious—the most valuable of metals. But you know, you can't eat gold or drink it. Like pound notes it has only symbolic value.

Because gold is a symbol of something so important and basic as the sun—something without which we'd all die—it has a religious significance as well. In the last book of the Bible, the perfect city is said to be made of pure gold. Of all the colours you see in churches, the gold on white is the one reserved for the most significant festivals.

And gold is always a symbol of the self. Not the self of selfishness, but that true self, that bit in the middle of us if you like that makes you into you and me into me. So when the alchemists, those strange men part scientist part priest, tried to make gold out of the other metals like copper, tin and mercury, that was just a code a secret language for what their craft was really about—the discovery and understanding of our innermost being—our self.

Heavenly Father, teach us to understand ourselves so that we are not ruled by either unworthy desires or by what others might say about us. Amen.

Religious Christmas Cards

In a large store there was a sign. It said 'Religious Christmas Cards.' What on earth could it mean? Aren't all Christmas cards religious because this is the time of year when we celebrate a religious festival—the birth of Christ?

Well, of course, we know what the sign really meant. Just that as well as cards showing robins and reindeers and Santa Claus, the shop had some which pictured the baby Jesus and Mary his mother, shepherds, kings and the manger.

Doesn't it seem sometimes that these two sorts of cards indicate two sorts of Christmas? There's Christmas for the religious person which is about getting up early on Christmas morning and striding out in the cold to church in order to give thanks for the birth of the Saviour.

Then there's Christmas for another sort of person. He likes to buy lots of presents, to decorate the front room with tinsel and a Christmas tree and to think about snow and sleigh bells and Santa.

Some religious people object to what they call 'the commercialization of Christmas'—the coloured lights in the streets, the Bing Crosby songs about snow and all the advertising which encourages us to make this time of the year into an orgy of spending.

Certainly they have a point. Shops shouldn't use Christmas as an excuse to exploit people. But then shops shouldn't exploit people at any other time either. But there are folk who gain and give a lot of pleasure by letting their hair down a bit at Christmas and by spending a bit more on pleasurable items.

The traditional religious Christmas doesn't carry a lot of meaning for many people. It doesn't seem to inspire them like it used to. So is there anything really wrong in enjoying the other side of Christmas—the toys, the tinsel and the television Christmas variety shows?

In a way the non-religious person's Christmas is every bit as religious as the churchgoer's. He would no more dream of forgetting the decorations than the religious person would miss hearing the Christmas gospel.

Perhaps both these forms of observance are just as valuable. They can both be the means of spreading goodwill. And that was the angels' song after all. 'Peace on earth; goodwill to men.'

Heavenly Father, thankyou for Christmas time. For the birth of your Son. And help us as we open our presents and celebrate this joyful occasion to spread goodwill among our neighbours. Amen.

Religion and Politics

You might have heard people say that religion should be kept out of politics and politics out of religion because they don't mix. Certainly these two subjects probably cause more argument, and fighting even, than any others. Men and women have fought political wars on religious bases for thousands of years. In our own day we need look no further than Northern Ireland in order to see violence and misery which is at least partly caused by religious and sectarian disagreement.

On one level it may be true that religion and politics shouldn't mix. That's on the level of party politics. It would be very difficult to say that someone couldn't be a true Christian unless he was also a member of the Conservative, Labour, or Liberal Party. A few people do try to make this claim, but it's hard to think it's generated by anything other than narrow prejudice in politics and a misunderstanding of the nature of religion.

In another way it's absolutely true that religion and politics can't be divorced from one another. Ever since Constantine made Christianity the state religion of the Roman Empire, the Church and therefore religion itself has been closely bound up with the secular authority.

In this country today, the Church of England is called the Established Church. The Queen in its Head. Prayers are said in both Houses of Parliament. Our monarchs are crowned in the Abbey. So in this sense there is a very definite mixture of politics and religion. This isn't a party political affair, of course, since all the parliamentary parties accept the authority of the Queen and the link between the religious and secular life of the nation.

But could it ever be wrong for a Christian or any person of a good religious conscience to belong to any particular political party. After all it seems a pretty basic right for anyone to make his own political allegiances. Isn't that why we have the secrecy of the ballot box?

It would be very difficult to see how anyone of Christian persuasion could justify support for the Nazi Party in Germany during the Second World War. How could Hitler's monstrous doctrines of hatred and persecution be squared with the ideal of Christian love? And it may be that there are extreme politics today of the left and the right which Christians ought not to support. But 'Pray before you vote' is a good slogan. Religion and politics are both concerned with people and so on some occasions they are bound to come into contact with each other.

Almighty God, help us to work together for the good of all people and the more complete understanding of your will. Amen.

Satan: Counsel for the Prosecution

Pantomime teaches us that the devil is a rather ugly creature with horns and a tail. He lives in an inferno called Hell and makes all his prisoners stoke the fires there. It's an amazing image but it's not true of course.

Other books and films like 'The Exorcist', 'The Omen' and 'The Devil Rides Out' give quite a different impression of Satan. In these works he's a much more sinister character, the embodiment of the power of evil. Able to possess people in body and soul. To torment and to damn.

This devil is the opposite of God. He's the power of darkness and evil while God is the power of light and goodness. And it's often suggested that God and the devil are constantly at war with each other. An eternal fight for supremacy. And that men and women are agents or instruments like chessmen in this battle.

But there's also a much older and more realistic tradition about who the devil is. In the book of Job and in Goethe's 'Faust' he's God's agent—a being with a special job to do. And that job is something like Counsel for the Prosecution. It's his job to find fault with God's world and to try and test men and women. This is a view which is in much closer accord with the Christian idea of God as the supreme and only creator. For if God and the devil are really eternal opposing powers then presumably the devil is God's equal. And that could mean that he might even win the ultimate war of the angels of light against the demons of darkness. And that evil eventually prevails.

This is quite contrary to Christian thought which says that God alone is the creator of all things. He even made the devil and gave him a particular job to do. The alternative is to believe that the devil created himself and that makes him equal with God.

Nowhere in Christian tradition is the devil made God's equal. Fallen Angel? Perhaps. Wicked Spirit? Maybe. The legend which makes him out to be Counsel for the Prosecution could be nearest the truth.

Heavenly Father, we worship you and give you thanks as the creator of all things. Help us to resist evil and to do good. Give us special strength when we are tested and tempted. Amen.

School-speak and Religious Language

'Busybodies', 'Nincompoops' and 'Clowns'. This isn't to insult you as a start to the day only to say that here are examples of three words that you'll hear only in schools—or at least only in schools do they carry a particular and special meaning that everyone recognizes.

There are lots of words and expressions like these. Phrases like 'prick up your ears', 'had better watch your step' etc sound as though they were invented in school corridors. You might think there's a whole language that belongs almost exclusively to school life. And you'd probably be right. We could call this language 'school-speak'. It's used all the time by teachers and pupils alike. And yet you wouldn't dream of using it anywhere else.

A philosopher called Ludwig Wittgenstein once said, 'Create a language and you create a world.' How true that is. Apart from the specialized languages of the arts and science, there are systems of talk connected with all our different activities. Think of the languages of pop-music or of football. There are words and phrases which belong there and nowhere else.

So we live in many worlds and not just in the one. Sometimes we're in the world of work and study; on other occasions we're in the universe of leisure and play. And in each situation we use quite different groups of expressions.

There is of course a religious language. Words like 'God', 'Heaven', 'Sin', 'Grace', 'Forgiveness' etc. And in a much narrower way there are the old fashioned religious words like 'Thee' and 'Thou', 'Thine' and 'Ye'. A lot of people think we should abolish this old way of talking in church or in our hymns and prayers. Some have even written new services which leave the old words out completely. They argue that people will understand modern words better and that 'Thee' and 'Thou' just confuse everybody.

Perhaps they have a point. But might it not also be possible that people understand religious words in a religious context—that is when they're praying and singing hymns. After all, teachers and pupils understand school-speak well enough.

And might it not also be true that if we remove so-called religious words from our vocabulary that we take away part of a religious sense or experience—because our religious language creates a religious world?

Heavenly Father, thankyou for the gift of language. Help us in our search for the right word in our conversation and writing. Amen.

Seasons in the Playground

Everyone knows about the main seasons of the year because there are holidays attached to them. Christmas, Easter and summer etc. And we have celebrations of these occasions in school. The nativity or a carol service; an Easter play; the harvest festival. They all occur on special days and you can plan for them and mark down the dates in your diary or on a calendar.

But there are other seasons. These belong in the playground and, outside school, on bits of spare land, parks and recreation grounds all over the country. There's no timetable for these; no date you can put in your diaries. These are the marbles season, the whip and top and hopscotch season, and the conker season.

Now nobody jumps out from behind a bush and holds out a sign saying 'It's February. Get on with the whips and tops!' And yet every year at this time these particular toys and pastimes come into fashion. Small whips and brightly chalked tops.

Later in the year conkers appear. Everywhere you go there are lads with horse chestnuts on bits of string. Some harden and toughen them by leaving them overnight in vinegar.

The amazing thing is that all these seasons begin and end without announcement, without written timetables. But that doesn't mean they're vague seasons—far from it. You try playing whip and top in August and your friends will think you're crazy. And they'll probably tell you so to.

All this seems to show that we're all very much ruled by custom, tradition and habit. What explanation can there be for what appears to be a sudden and spontaneous outbreak of conkers and hopscotch which stops as abruptly as it started—without signal, without warning? It's not as though anyone is forced into these activities by the advertising industry.

Well, maybe it's part of our history. Something which goes very deep, like Christmas and Guy Fawkes Night. An event we just couldn't miss. Whatever cause we might find for these seasonal games, they are a good thing, for they give us yet more opportunity to meet together and enjoy the fellowship of shared leisure.

Almighty God, thankyou for the order of the times and seasons; for Christmas and Easter; Summer and the New Year. Thankyou as well for the unscripted seasons of playground games and for giving us our friends. Amen.

Sensory Deprivation

Most of us have never been in absolute dark and silence. Bedrooms can be pretty quiet and gloomy in the middle of the night. And graveyards are spooky and still. But for absolute blackness and quiet we have to go to an artificially created room which psychologists use for their experiments on our senses.

Such rooms do exist and subjects enter them, voluntarily of course, in order to discover what a complete lack of external stimulus does to the human mind. In these places there's neither sound nor light. So what effect does it have on the courageous characters who dare enter?

Well, most people who've tried the experiment say that after a while in the dark room they began to have hallucinations—to see and hear things that weren't there at all really. It looks as if the human mind faced with the absence of all appearances needs to invent a world for itself. And perhaps that accounts for the hallucinations.

We've all heard our stomach give the odd rumble just before lunch, but for the most of the time we're not conscious of our inward bodily processes. You can't hear your heart beat or your eyelids blink. But in the black room in conditions which the psychologists call 'sensory deprivation' all our quietest bodily processes can be heard in action. Senses of taste return strongly as well. One man reported that, after he'd been in the black room for about fifteen minutes, he suddenly tasted very strongly the oysters he'd eaten the day before.

Of course it doesn't do to keep people in sensory deprivation chambers for too long. They soon become anxious and distressed. Perhaps that shows how much we really need one another however much we like to claim that we like to be on our own.

But one of the most interesting aspects of this experiment is the awareness which it creates of a whole world going on inside us—a world we usually take for granted but without which we wouldn't be alive at all.

Heavenly Father, thankyou for making us as bodies which sustain themselves without our having to think about it all the time. And bless those who seek to discover more about the inner workings of human beings in mind and body so that we may learn to cure the sick and preserve health. Amen.

She's Leaving Home

In the 1960s 'The Beatles' pop group brought out a record called 'She's Leaving Home'. It was about a teenage girl who walked out on her parents and all her past life in the early hours of the morning. And it was also about the thoughts about her which haunted her parents as they lay in bed.

They were very sad wondering why their daughter should leave them in this dramatic way. 'We gave her all of our life; everything money can buy' they said to themselves. And so why should she go so suddenly? Hadn't they, like so many parents, offered her all they had? Done everything for their child? Why does she repay them in such an apparently cruel and ungrateful fashion?

It's generally true that relationships between parents and children, boyfriends and girlfriends, husbands and wives don't break down *suddenly* at all. The actual act of parting may seem an abrupt event, but it's likely that the causes of the parting had been building up over a long period.

Maybe the parents of that girl in the Beatles' song hadn't noticed that her particular needs were changing. She was growing up. Perhaps searching for a greater degree of independence from the tightly knit family group. More freedom over her hours for coming in and going out. Her own choice of friends and career. Because her parents, out of loving but misguided concern for her, denied her many of these things—denied her the right to be herself—she gradually built up to that point of no return when the break between daughter and parents became final.

It seems to be a universal truth that we can't take relationships for granted and expect them to be all right. We need to work hard at our friendships. To make an effort to see the other person's needs and point of view. And this is true whether we're talking about boyfriends, girlfriends, mothers, fathers, aunts, uncles, teachers, pupils or anyone else. It needs a constant attempt to anticipate the wishes of our parents or our friends if we're to avoid that awful moment when there's no talking anymore because there's no relationship left.

Almighty Father, help us to understand one another and to appreciate the different needs of different people. Amen.

Soma—The Miracle Drug

If you're ever feeling depressed, think what a perfect world might be like. Delightful food and drink, no money problems, a satisfying job, tireless energy. And then there'd be an endless diversity of entertainments for leisure time. Of course, perfect health and tons of energy would be needed as well. You can have all these in *Brave New World*—a novel by Aldous Huxley.

Even in an ideal world though it's just possible you might occasionally lose your temper or get a bit angry with one of your friends. Don't worry. Huxley's world takes care of that. There's a harmless drug you see called 'Soma'. Take a gramme and all's well. Instant interior sunshine. Sour moods and evil tempers vanish. No need to get annoyed—ever. Just take a speck of Soma. As Huxley says, 'A gramme is better than a damn.'

What wonderful advantages to this sort of world. No arguments, fights or wars. Everybody living in peace and harmony. Society working as smoothly as a well-oiled machine. What a welcome change this would be from our crazy mixed-up and anxious world.

And yet there's something about *Brave New World* that's completely unsatisfactory. Huxley himself introduces a character called 'the savage' in order to show us how it's possible to be unhappy even in a so called perfect world. 'The savage' isn't really a savage at all. He's an ordinary man and his objection to Brave New World is that it's taken away all possibility of choice and decision and therefore destroyed the spirit of mankind. In the perfect world you don't have the opportunity to be unhappy or unsatisfied, so you don't have the chance to struggle and strive.

Of course, it would be a great blessing to be able to take a gramme of something to stop our tempers rising at inconvenient moments. But Brave New World keeps us quiet all the time. Soma stops us arguing, questioning and becoming aggressive on those occasions when we need to stir things up. Soma costs nothing except our humanity. We weren't built as robots. Men and women are more than machines. And that's worth remembering when we're tempted by delusions of a perfect world.

Almighty God, give us the courage to seek to change those things which are in need of change, and to strive constantly to make the world a place where men and women consider more the needs of others before their own. Amen.

Something Awful From the Cellar

There's a story about a lad called Timothy and he's going to spend a Saturday night at home with his best friend, Brian. His parents are going out for the evening because it's their wedding anniversary. Anyway Timothy doesn't mind because Brian will come round and they'll play 'Cluedo' for a while, then watch 'Match of the Day'.

But on Saturday morning Brian's mother telephones to say that Brian won't be able to come round because he's got chicken pox. Timothy says he doesn't care too much, though he's a bit disappointed he'll still be able to watch the television and have a quiet read.

Come the evening and Tim's mum and dad are ready to go out celebrating. They've left Timothy some money to buy some chicken and chips from the corner take-away. They'll be back at about half past eleven.

'Are you OK, Tim?' his dad asks.

'Course I am,' says Tim.

'Sorry Brian couldn't come.'

'Oh that's all right. I'll read and watch the football.'

So they go out. And quite suddenly everything's different. It's so quiet. Nothing's moving. You could almost believe that the table, the chairs, the sofa, the television set even, were looking at Timothy and waiting. Waiting perhaps for him to do something.

Tim does something all right. He gets up and goes to the kitchen for one of those biscuits that have got chocolate on one side. As he puts the lid back on the tin, he thinks he hears something else and feels a little bit lonely. But he goes back with the biscuit and a tin of lemonade and sits in the front room looking out of the window. There's nothing to be afraid of. It's still light even.

Suddenly, there's the beginning of a slow heavy clump. Something's coming up the cellar steps. No there isn't. It stops. Then suddenly it starts again. Timothy becomes beside himself with panic. He daren't move. He can't sit still. His heart pounds like a pneumatic drill.

The clump, clump of the stair climbing tread stops. There's a crash as the cellar door bursts open. After a short pause, steps can be heard moving from the top of the stairs to the front room. Timothy is so terrified he's dizzy. As he's on the very point of passing out with fear, in the doorway opposite appears a man, if 'man' be the right word. Eight feet tall and draped in seaweed. With massive, prominent teeth of rotting vicious yellow and staring, red eyes. . . .

We all like this kind of thing in a way. It's worth asking the question, 'Why do people enjoy being scared out of their wits?'

Heavenly Father, thankyou for entertainment in all its various forms and for those who invent and act out stories for our amusement. Amen.

The Space Between the Notes

Young people have always liked lively music; jazz, rock 'n roll, reggae— [illegible] different varieties. It's probably something to do with youth and energy. Perhaps when you get a bit older you might like something a bit more gentle. Some of you are even now very fond of so called 'classical music', of Mozart, Beethoven, Bach and the others.

But it would be a mistake to think that all classical music is tuneless and 'all the same'. We're used to finding attractive melodies of instant appeal in Beethoven and Tchaikovsky—the makers of commercials for television know all about our love of these. They've even got Beethoven's Pastoral Symphony into a perfume advertisement; and the Mozart C major piano concerto into promoting the sale of coal. But a lot of twentieth-century classical music doesn't seem to have those tunes that appeal so immediately. There is a lot of difference between a string quartet by Haydn and one by Bartok.

Some people think that modern composers—men like Stockhausen and Messiaen have gone too far. Not only have they rejected tunes but they've also thrown out all the old-fashioned harmonies that go to make up the popular classics we love so well. Someone once said of a piece by Karlheinz Stockhausen that it was just like the banging of dustbin lids. Really, though, we need to regard modern composers in a different way before we can enjoy them properly.

But there's one piece of music, though I don't know whether you can rightly call it music, which has outraged thousands of people. It's supposed to be a piece for piano lasting exactly four minutes and thirty-three seconds. And this is what happens. The concert lovers are in the hall. The piano is in the middle of the stage. Right on time in comes the pianist in full evening dress. Amid expectation he sits at the piano, fingers poised, for exactly four minutes thirty-three seconds. But he doesn't play a note. Then he gets up, bows to the audience and leaves the stage—having played nothing.

What a trick you might say! What a swindle! I could do that and there's that fellow getting paid for it! Can you think of why John Cage wrote or didn't write (if you see what I mean) that piece for piano? Perhaps it was to tell us in a dramatic form that music doesn't just consist of notes, but of the spaces of silence between the notes. In a musical composition short periods of silence of varying lengths are as necessary to the overall effect as the notes themselves.

Almighty God, we thank you for music and musicians. For music that enlivens; music that inspires; music that teaches; music that comforts. Help us to appreciate the partnership of silence and sound. Amen.

Spencer's Ill-spent Youth

Herbert Spencer, philosopher and natural scientist once said that someone had remarked to him 'Billiards was the sign of an ill-spent youth.' It's difficult to believe that there's anything specially evil about billiards. In fact Mozart used to play. So whoever remarked to Spencer that billiards was the sign of an ill-spent youth probably thought that all games—maybe all indoor games anyway—were a waste of time.

And yet we get such enjoyment from leisure occupations which perhaps seem to have no particular end in themselves—no final product we can look at and admire or judge. Billiards. Snooker. Cards. 'Scrabble'. 'Monopoly'. Table-tennis. What's wrong with these?

Maybe the answer is that there's nothing wrong with them; only something a little wrong with the ideas of those who wish to condemn them—to call them a waste of time.

Some people are unable to be happy unless they're working. Leisure and play make them feel guilty—as if they're misusing time by taking a break from the daily routine and going along for a game of billiards, or even settling in front of the television for an hour's relaxation over a comedy film.

Now, of course, it takes a great deal of self-discipline to work consistently hard—to do yout stint every day. And no one should complain about those folk who take pleasure in a task well completed. And work on this regular basis is absolutely necessary for the proper working of our society. Imagine the fine state we'd be in if nobody ever turned up for work at the right time.

But how much easier it is to apply yourself to hard work if you also allow yourself leisure. We all know the saying about all work and no play making Jack a dull boy. And it's true. At its best leisure—billiards, snakes and ladders or what you will is recreation. And recreation is re-creation: making ourselves new again for another stab at the daily routine.

Heavenly Father, help us so to work that we are satisfied in what we do, and to use our leisure to refresh and recreate ourselves. Amen.

Spots and Blemishes

You must have read those magazines for teenagers which have long articles and thousands of adverts all about how to make yourself beautiful. We're all supposed to buy a certain kind of soap, talcum powder or hairdressing. And even men aren't immune; there's after shave, pre-shave cologne and deodorants galore.

And there are the anxious titters. You know the kind of thing: 'I've met this gorgeous boy at our youth club. He's great and he likes motor-bikes and football and things. And he's ever so kind. But I'm scared he won't look at me because I've got spots on my face.' And it's signed 'Worried, Wimbledon.'

Whatever is she going to do? How will she attract the boy of her dreams when she's got dots on her face? Then there's the reply isn't there: 'Dear Worried. Wimbledon, It's quite usual for people of your age to develop acne. There's nothing much you can do really except to wash your face regularly. And try not to be too anxious. If your heartthrob is sincere he'll like you—spots and all.'

Well really! Just what are these magazines trying to do? On the one hand they say that it's not terribly important how you look as long as you're nice and clean. Then on the other hand they're after persuading you by their fancy adverts to spend all your money on cosmetics. There's a contradiction here.

It's not that you shouldn't try and make yourself look attractive. Everybody feels better when they know they're looking their best. It's simply that magazines shouldn't be allowed to exploit the anxiety and self-consciousness we all share about our appearance at one time or another.

And while it's nice to be able to get rid of spots and blemishes, looking like a model or film star isn't the most important thing—not by a long way. It's better to be yourself—not to conform to the plastic model that a lot of advertisements urge us towards—and to realize that you're an individual person in your own right. And like everybody else you've got many attractive characteristics and some which are less so.

It's called being human.

Heavenly Father, You make us in your own image. Give us the courage to be ourselves. Amen.

Spring and Port Wine

An enchanting film, made in a northern industrial town, is called 'Spring and Port Wine'. It's been on release a good many years and has ever been presented on the television. 'Spring and Port Wine' is about an ordinary working-class family who live in Bolton. The father, head of the household, is a most just and virtuous man. He cares deeply for his family and works hard to support them.

He's also a religious person. And he brings his religious commitment very firmly to bear on family life. So there's always grace said before meals and Bible reading on Sundays. The father derives his justice and fairness from rules—some of which he gets from the Bible and others he subscribes to as valid in that they promote respect and dignity.

He observes these rules absolutely. Having made a decision he'll never go back on it. Once in the film this caused great distress in the family because he insisted that one of his children should get nothing else to eat until the refused and dreaded herring had been consumed. So the fish was brought out day after day, meal after meal until it stank. The father's insistence on inflexible rules threatened to split his family apart.

This isn't to say that rules are therefore evil. Without rules no society could survive. No family. No school. But there have to be times when rules are amended, altered or quite straightforwardly ignored in the light of circumstances.

For an extreme example, suppose a school field had been declared 'out of bounds' by the head teacher. Now there's a fire in the prefabricated cricket pavillion in the corner of that field, and there's no way of putting the fire out without treading on the grass. Certainly the headteacher wouldn't punish an enthusiastic fire-fighter who was standing on the field throwing buckets of water on the blaze.

If he did, he'd be as inflexible as the father in 'Spring and Port Wine'. One would lose his pavilion, the other perhaps his family. And this doesn't mean that we can just disobey rules when we like. No. For the most part they should be obeyed because they're for the common good. It's only when they threaten that common good that we should change them.

Heavenly Father, your son taught us that the law of love is greater than the might of law. Help us always to act in the common good. Amen.

A Sure Stronghold

Do you think of God as an old man in the sky? Perhaps not. But it's amazing to discover how many people do have such a childish idea of God. A kindly grandparent with a white beard resting on top of the clouds. There are more sophisticated, perhaps more realistic and valuable images of God than that one.

Some imagine him to be an invisible spirit who exists in all places and in all times. So that it makes sense to say 'God exists six inches above my head.' Another image of God is a divine spark in the middle of every human being. So that makes sense of Jesus' saying about loving God and loving your neighbour amounting to the same thing.

We can use any particular picture which we find sensible and helpful, because all our talk about God is bound to be metaphorical—in terms of something else—simply because no one has ever seen him as he is. One of the best pictures is that of God as Father—someone Jesus told us we can turn to with all our needs and cares. A kind Father, an understanding Father.

Martin Luther refers to God as a safe castle–'Ein Feste Burg'. It may strike us as odd to think of God as a castle. But that German phrase also means a sure stronghold. Somewhere absolutely safe.

Perhaps it's not such a strange picture after all. Imagine for a moment some of the benefits which a castle, a stronghold gives. Warmth. Comfort. Safety. Light. Rest. Perhaps even turrets—a balcony from which to view the world.

If God is real, if the word 'God' means anything at all then he is like a castle in many ways. He gives us the promise of his comfort whenever we feel in need of it. He himself is secure and so makes us secure. He is strong and everlasting just like those ancient castles at York or Edinburgh which look as if they're meant for eternity.

In the end all our pictures of God are inadequate. They rely on human imagination and mortal language. But the idea of one who is 'A Safe Stronghold' is worth a thought—even a thought of one as good as Martin Luther.

Almighty God, be our stronghold in times when we are afraid, our strength when we're distressed. Amen.

Technical Types

Are you an expert on very detailed analysis of complex and complicated documents? Most of us would say 'No' in answer to that question. And secretly we envy the lawyer who can make sense out of page after page of that incomprehensible legal jargon. Or the accountant who's able to glance at a sheet of figures and tell straight away whether the company's books he's studying are in the black or the red.

Most of us wouldn't lay claim to this kind of expertise. 'Oh I'm not very good at figures' and 'It's all Greek to me' are sentences which have passed into our language like clichés. And that's because so many people are less confident about their own expertise.

Perhaps the very image of the obscure world of the experts is the financial page in the so called serious daily and weekly newspapers. Here there are tables of share prices written in such tiny print you can hardly read them. And strange phrases like 'The F. T. all share index', 'Actuaries', 'Gilts' and 'Fiscal drag'. How can anyone make sense of all this? Whoever can must be a very great expert.

And yet there are at least two areas of interest in our newspapers which are every bit as complex as the financial page but which lots of ordinary folk can read like the back of a bus ticket.

First there's the cricket reports. Have you ever stopped to wonder how an eleven year old boy's head could possibly be large enough to include such items as 'googlies', 'forward short leg' or to give it its more humorous title 'silly mid on'?

Then there's the averages, the calculation of bonus points and the law about the follow on.

For older people who like a bit of a gamble there's the racing page. Now we're really in deep water. How can anyone cope with:

'0300113 RED KNIGHT (HODGES) 9–7 brackets 7
impd last tim out (Carson)—heavy 100–8'?

But every morning thousands of ordinary men digest pages of this in a matter of minutes during the tea break. It goes to show at least two things. People are not as ignorant as they think they are. And you can understand anything at all if you're interested enough.

Almighty God, lead us away from narrow-mindedness and into an understanding of the many and varied areas of knowledge which challenge our perseverance. Amen.

The Temple and the Tent

In the middle of Liverpool there are two large cathedrals. One's the Church of England's property, and its got the longest aisle of any church in the country. The other's a modern structure and it belongs to the Roman Catholics.

Now both buildings cost a great deal of money to build. The Church of England's place isn't even finished yet and it was begun more than fifty years ago. Many people, looking at poverty and unemployment in Liverpool, come straight out and say that the money for building these two enormous cathedrals could have been better spent on something else. Something more urgent. Perhaps care of the elderly.

They argue that God can be worshipped in much greater simplicity and at far less cost in prefabricated buildings, in more economical public halls and even in private houses. Such expense as the Liverpool cathedrals involved is a monstrous waste of resources, or so it is said.

You may have your own opinions about who should pay for church buildings and how much should be spent in their upkeep. But you might be surprised to learn that it's an age old problem. People have been talking about this issue for hundreds, even thousands of years.

The Israelites, for instance, when they were wandering in the wilderness, worshipped God in a tent which they carried around with them. And when they eventually settled in the promised land there were those among them who said that if a tent had been good enough in the wilderness it would be just as good in Canaan.

But others argued that belief in God and all the powerful religious feelings and experiences which often go with that belief demand that men and women give something of the very best of their art and science in praise and thanksgiving. And so the mighty—and incredibly expensive—temple of Solomon was constructed.

Many ordinary folk in Liverpool think as the builders of King Solomon's temple thought—that, of course you can worship God in a tent, or even in the open air, but that it's fitting to have a beautiful temple as well. You must make up your minds where you stand on this issue.

Heavenly Father, help us to use our time, our skills and our money for good purposes and deliver from habits of wastefulness. Amen.

Thinking or Feeling

You know how it's often said of someone that he has an 'ear for music' or that someone else, a painter perhaps, has an 'eye for beauty'. Football players frequently find themselves described in the sports pages as men who've got 'magic feet'. Detectives, as if they really were bloodhounds, are said to have 'a nose for crime'—as steeplejacks have a 'head for heights'.

And it's all good, picturesque, descriptive language. But not all human occupations can be so neatly labelled. For instance, when we come to consider faith or religion. What convenient metaphor might we invent here?

It's not quite so easy. But there's one distinction we can make. And that's between those who think religion is a matter for the intellect and others who think it has more to do with emotion. The difference between the response of the mind and the response of the heart. In short the distinction between thinking and feeling.

Those who see religious belief as an intellectual exercise, often point to the need to see the universe as a rational and logical order and consequently argue that its creator should be approached in a careful, intellectual way. There are the scholars who go in for proofs or at least evidences of God's existence.

But there are other points of view. That of Samuel Taylor Coleridge for example who said that he was weary of evidences for the existence of God. He wanted men and women to feel the presence of God—to be aware of him through the emotions.

We might ask whether one approach is right and the other wrong or whether we can have a vision of God by either method and by both. It's certainly a fact that emotion plays a large part in the religious faith of many, while for others belief is a matter of careful reasoning and intellectual attention.

Perhaps both approaches have something different to offer at different times—in the same way that sometimes we turn for truth to an equation and at other times we seek out a poem.

Heavenly Father, help us to keep a balance between thinking and feeling so that our emotions are ordered and our thoughts are imaginative. Amen.

The Three Pillars

Sometimes when people think of opera they imagine great fat ladies taking deep breaths and making all kinds of funny noises. I used to think like this, and it's true that a lot of operas seem to have very melodramatic plots—stories that you can't believe in set to music that you can't abide.

But there's at least one opera that's quite different. In fact when I first saw it performed it didn't seem like a boring opera at all—it was more like a pantomine. It's called 'The Magic Flute' and it was first heard in September 1791. You may have heard of it and know that it was written by Mozart not long before he died.

Well there are all kinds of creatures in it—everything that seems to be made for a pantomime or a fairy story. There's a snake and a bird catcher; a magician and an Egyptian temple; soldiers and spirits and many more strange beings.

In a way 'The Magic Flute' is a love story, and as in all love stories there's a handsome prince and a princess. And of course the princess has a wicked mother—she's called the Queen of the Night. What a title! What a name! How frightening—The Queen of the Night.

Anyway, the hero Prince Tamino sets out to rescue her daughter Pamina from the castle of an evil magician. Tamino is very much in love with Pamina and not at all scared even when he comes to the very gateway of the evil magician Sarastro. In a courtyard he sees three pillars and on them are carved strange words in a foreign language. When these words are translated for Tamino he learns that they mean 'work', 'happiness' and 'artistry'. Only later when he discovers that Sarastro is not wicked after all, but the kindly High Priest of the Temple of Wisdom, does Tamino learn the real meaning of these strange words.

You see, The Queen of the Night had lied to him. Tamino could only really be united with the beautiful Pamina when he'd come to appreciate that Work, Happiness and Artistry are three beautiful and worthwhile things which belong together.

So he was instructed by Sarastro and the other priests and finally. The Queen of the Night was overthrown and Tamino lived happily ever after with his princess in the Temple of Wisdom.

Heavenly Father, help us in our work to make beautiful things. And let other people and ourselves find true happiness through them. Amen.

Union of the Opposites

Have you noticed how every word and every idea carries within it the sense of its own opposite? So we can't think of 'light' without also thinking of 'darkness', of 'day' without 'night', of 'calm' without 'storm', 'heat' without 'cold' and so on. No doubt you can think of many more examples.

In a way this is obvious, but in another sense it's really quite odd and needs some thinking about—especially in the use of words which have to do with human activities like 'giving' and 'getting'; 'loving' and 'hating'; 'creating' and 'destroying.'

Perhaps we've all felt jealous at one time or another. And of course you know that jealousy is called 'the green-eyed monster.' Now it's very damaging to be jealous and here's why. If you have a friend and you see him, or perhaps her going around or spending a lot of time with somebody else, how awful you feel. The first instinct is to lash out or sulk, in some way to take it out of your friend, to punish him for not taking enough notice of you and instead attending far too closely to someone else.

But here's why this is damaging for far from bringing your friend back to you, it's far more likely that such surly behaviour will drive him further away. This kind of behaviour is called possessiveness and it ends with the would be possessor having nothing at all. You can't own or possess other people. If you try you'll finish up by becoming very unhappy and lonely. Ask anyone who's tried to win back a boy-friend/girlfriend through sulking or moody behaviour.

And it's the same with all other emotions. If someone really dislikes you—hates you even—and you reply by hating in return, you'll only make the situation worse because you'll use up a lot of energy hating and succeed in making yourself miserable in the process.

Perhaps this is where Jesus' instruction that we should love our enemies and do good to those who are spiteful to us really makes sense. It's only by acting in the opposite way to that in which our first inclinations lead us that we can turn a bad situation into a good one and bring happiness out of evil. Of course it's not easy. Nobody ever says it is. But just think about it when you feel the next flush of jealousy.

Heavenly Father, teach us to do good to those who use us spitefully and to repay evil with good and so fulfil the commandment of your son our Lord Jesus Christ. Amen.

Unwelcome Enthusiasm

It's very odd how the meanings of words can change so much over the years. Of course words don't alter their meanings suddenly. It takes centuries sometimes. But meanings do change. Take for instance the word 'indifferent'. This used to mean 'impartial'—making no difference in attitude towards one thing or another. And so in the Prayer Book when it says, '. . . truly and indifferently minister justice to the punishment of wickedness' it doesn't mean taking no different circumstances into account. It means administering the same justice to all people regardless of their rank or wealth. In other words acting impartially.

Nowadays, though, 'indifferent' means something like not caring one way or the other. 'Do you want jam sponge or rice pudding?' Answer: 'It doesn't matter; I'm indifferent about desserts.'

Another word that's changed is 'prevent.' There's a prayer that begins 'Prevent us O Lord in all our doings. . .'. How extraordinary! Fancy praying that God will prevent us in our activities. Well it didn't mean that originally. It meant 'Go before' or 'Lead'. Perhaps you can think of other examples.

One word that's changed beyond recognition is 'enthusiasm'. We know how we use it these days. We talk about people having enthusiasm—keenness and interest. Enthusiasm, perhaps, for a football team. Even enthusiasm for work. And we think enthusiasm is a good thing. A quality to be cultivated and admired. Teachers are always encouraging enthusiasm.

But it wasn't always so. At the beginning of the nineteenth century enthusiasm was almost a crime. Those who showed spirit, particularly in political and social affairs were thought to be very dangerous. It's hardly surprising really, since at that time everybody was feeling the upheaval of the French Revolution and would do almost anything for a quiet life. Enthusiasm was looked upon as an undesirable quality usually possessed by those who believed in rocking the boat—changing the existing order.

This teaches us yet again that language is a living and changing thing. Perhaps it also makes us think carefully about which things should claim our enthusiasm. The best and most worthwhile enthusiasm is that for a cause we've thought about seriously. It's easy to play follow my leader or to jump on bandwaggons. It's more demanding but more rewarding to think things out for ourselves.

Almighty God, help us to use our minds properly; to measure with reason the justice of causes we are called upon to support. And give us the enthusiasm to follow our decisions with boldness. Amen.

Sw 25/1/79

Victoria, Gladstone and the Public Meeting

Nearly all prominent politicians manage to get themselves known as the authors of an original phrase or two. Lloyd George used to advertise his national insurance scheme with the phrase 'ninepence for fourpence'. Churchill talked of 'blood, toil, tears and sweat' in the dark days of the war and he first called the Royal Air Force 'The Few'.

Harold Macmillan was famous for his electioneering slogan 'You've never had it so good' while Harold Wilson is remembered for 'A week is a long time in politics' and 'A tightly knit group of politically motivated men'.

Politics really is a rather dour and dull affair. MPs sit up half the night on tedious committee meetings. Local councillors are obliged to talk about the most boring subjects like the drains, the water supply and the buses running on time. The Queen's Speech and the Opening of Parliament are the icing on what is a pretty ordinary sort of cake.

So it's good when a politician brightens up the proceedings by introducing a choice and evocative phrase to two. Generally their language is almost forced to be that of the pedestrian and run-of-the-mill civil service document.

In the last century England had a Queen in Victoria who was quite a character herself and who frequently granted audience to the prime minister of the day. The best known of these were Mr Gladstone and Mr Disraeli. For the best part of twenty-five years they fought political battles with each other. And consequently Victoria got to know them well.

Disraeli she loved. He was, apparently, gentle and soft spoken, respectful and calm. But Gladstone, though a great statesman, wasn't altogether to Victoria's liking. She once said of him, 'He always talks to me as if he's addressing a public meeting.' Perhaps for all his political eminence Mr Gladstone couldn't help it. Maybe he was shy and needed to retreat into a kind of official language when he was speaking to the Queen. We'll never know for sure. But what we can learn from this little saying of Victoria's is that no one likes to be addressed as if he's an official gathering. Our conversation with one another should involve politeness and courtesy and—as far as our shyness allows—a touch of personal informality.

Heavenly Father, teach us to speak to one another as friends. Amen.

The Wellingtons That Leaked

When it gets into December, one of the nicest things to look forward to—apart from Christmas of course—is the snow. November's misty and damp, but then, if you're lucky, one day early in December, all the fog and damp has blown away, the pavements in the town are white and dry. And there's a nip in the air. The sky looks so grey and heavy you could believe it was going to fall in. Suddenly it seems to turn a little bit warmer—or is that just our imagination playing tricks—and it begins to snow. Slowly at first—sometimes the flakes appear to be retreating in a sort of idle meander back up into the sky. And you think it might stop, or worse still turn to rain. But it doesn't. And soon it's lying white and thick. And even the main streets seem quieter.

Marvellous if it's the school holidays when it snows because you can go out and play in it all day. Of course, you've got to put on an extra pair of thick socks to keep your toes warm. And, most important, wellington boots so you don't ruin your shoes. Now the first snow of winter can catch you unprepared. On with the socks and the wellingtons and out into the lovely whiteness. Making new tracks in the snow; hurling great lumps of the stuff at the concrete uprights of street lamps; feeling that coldness on the hands which almost seems to burn.

Only after you've been out there for a quarter of an hour or so do you begin to feel just a bit uncomfortable. The left foot seems damp and that extra woolly sock goes wet and heavy. Those wellingtons you've put on haven't been worn since last February and the long summer holiday has made you forget that the left boot leaks. But now what do you do? Do you leave your friends and come in for a warm bath and an early tea? Not likely! The snow's far too important to miss for the sake of a soggy sock. You stay out there and nurse the chilblains later.

And there's a difference between an adult and a child. Dad out shifting the snow and Mum on her way to the shops and finding their boots leaked would come home straight away and do something about it. But not so with boys and girls. That would spoil the magic that's part of being young during the first snow of winter.

Heavenly Father, thank you for gifts of natural beauty like the snow. Help us all, men and women, boys and girls to appreciate the beauty of nature. Guide us to be childlike but not childish. Amen.

Wesak

'Wesak'. What a strange word. It sounds like a combination of a detergent and an American television police series. But really it's quite a serious word. The name of a festival when Buddhists remember their founder Guatama whose other name—Buddha—means 'the enlightened one'.

Guatama was a Hindu prince and lived about five hundred years before Christ. What's so special about him is that he wasn't satisfied by the teachings of his native Hindu religion, so he went off on his own to try and discover the truth about God and the world.

After a long while, six years as the legend has it, Guatama arrived at a view of life which satisfied him. As his followers who are called 'Buddhists' say, 'He received enlightenment'.

Of course there are many lessons we could draw from Buddhism—a faith two thousand five hundred years old. There are the special doctrines and symbols like the eightfold path and the wheel of life. But perhaps one of the most interesting aspects of Guatama's story is the fact that he felt compelled to leave his home and riches, more than that leave behind his religious belief and set out to find his own way in the world and discover a meaning in life which would satisfy him.

This is a great puzzle. Why are some people able to accept the faith of their fathers and grandfathers without question? Why do others need to work everything out anew for themselves? A nineteenth-century thinker called William James divided believers into two groups; what he called 'the once born' and 'the twice born'. Most of us find sufficient in the religious teachings, customs and festivals of our own society to satisfy our needs. But some rare people seem to need to venture out, to explore new paths of faith for mankind. Whereas we ordinary folk may be 'once born' according to Willian James, Buddha is a shining example of those spiritual explorers we might call 'twice born'.

Heavenly Father, help us to learn from all that is valuable in the traditions of the past but always to be open to the new truths which you are teaching us in the present. Amen.

What Next?

Many of you like to watch science fiction programmes on the television and to read books like 'Twenty-thousand Leagues Under the Sea', 'War of the Worlds' or 'The Time Machine'. And of course these are filled with excitement. They're out of the ordinary, not talking about the world as it is in what sometimes seems its rather tedious and dreary existence—but about an imaginary world full of flying saucers, monsters, futuristic machines and weird plants.

There's a marvellous book by Olaf Stapledon called *Last and First Men.* It's written on a vast time scale. The early chapters deal with the period around 1914 and as each type or evolution of man takes place—first men, second men, third men etc—the book projects thousands of years into the future. Stapledon's book is jam-packed with excitement and adventure.

But the most fascinating thing about it is its preoccupation with the future—with what's going to happen next. Above everything else it's this that keeps you reading. And isn't this true about most science fiction and about men and women in general? We're fascinated by the idea of the future because we think that anything might happen—and, of course, we're right.

Theoretically, anything could happen. A world war—or a world government. Visitors from outer space. Strange plants taking over the world. And the great thing is nobody can say that science fiction stories aren't true. And that's because most of the events they talk about haven't happened yet. You can't say that something's false if it hasn't even had the chance to occur.

You know that Jesus told parables. Well, perhaps science fiction stories go together to make up a parable—a story with a meaning. And maybe the parable in science fiction tales is that we should keep an open mind about the future and not simply think that everything's going to go on in the way it's always gone in the past.

Not that we should immediately expect visitors from Jupiter. Just that yesterday's science fiction has an uncanny way of becoming today's science fact. Who would have thought—apart from the science fiction writers a hundred years ago—that one day men would fly to the moon?

Science fiction reveals the universe in an optimistic way. It tells us that however great today is, tomorrow will be yet more mysterious.

Heavenly Father, thankyou for the wonders of the universe. Help us to contribute to the future by thinking carefully about our actions in the present. Amen.

When the Night Light Went Out

Some young people are lucky because parents leave a small light on in the children's bedroom and the night doesn't seem half so frightening. Everyone has gone through a phase of being scared in the dark. It's difficult to find out just what's so weird about a bedroom when you're a child, alone in it, and it's dark.

Perhaps it's something to do with being alone. Children go to bed before their parents, so there's a sharp contrast between being one minute in the middle of a bright, lively, noisy downstairs room and the next moment in a quiet, still, dark upstairs place. And the stairs have something to do with it. They divide us from the rest of the company—put us on a level where we're alone.

So it's a comfort if you're eight years old and all on your own in a silent bedroom to have a night light. A friendly glow in the eerie darkness. It's a comfort even if you're older than eight; it's not just very young children who are afraid of the dark.

And there's something about night—apart from the darkness—which is quite different from the daytime. Many who would boldly pour scorn on the existence of ghosts in a conversation in the middle of the day wouldn't sound quite so confident late at night.

Then parents come to bed. And if you're unlucky enough to be still awake, you see the light go out. Suddenly silence and dark close in together. This is the really weird time. Furniture creaks. Familiar objects look sinister in the gloom. And there's something you can't make out towards the corner of the room. In the morning it turns out to be an old pullover—but what was it last midnight in the dark? An old pullover still. No doubt. But it didn't look like one.

Really there's nothing to be afraid of. Every morning is a reassurance that night is quite an ordinary phenomenon. But remembering what it's like to be scared in the dark ought to help us have more sympathy with our younger brothers and sisters when they're afraid. Darkness is a gentle cover to encourage sleep. But in the dark . . . on your own? That can be quite a different story.

Heavenly Father, thankyou for the day and for the night. Comfort us when we cannot go to sleep and drive away all fear at night-time. Amen.

White Dwarfs

How often do we judge the usefulness or value of a thing to be connected with it's size? We seem to think that everything from football grounds to plates of chips are to be prized according to how big they are. Of course, there is some value in size—if you're a wing forward in rugby or a centre back at football, then sheer height and strength count for quite a lot.

But we all know of tiny sportsmen who are outstanding in their performance. And many influential and powerful leaders of nations have been small men. Napoleon, conqueror of Europe, was a little chap. For what it's worth, so was Hitler. Einstein wasn't tall. St Paul was a short man.

This leads to the statement—often made by little fellows: 'Good stuff goes into little room.' No doubt there's some truth in it.

In the physical universe there are examples which might strike us as similar. We're always being told how vast other planets, star systems and galaxies are compared with the earth. All this sort of talk could make us quite small, or at least feel quite small and inferior.

But here's a strange truth. Deep in the universe there are stars called 'white dwarfs'. These aren't like ordinary stars, large, vast and brilliant. They're really quite tiny in comparison with most other stellar bodies. Yet the atoms they're made from are crushed together so closely that their weight is enormous in relation to their size.

If you detected a white dwarf from a distance, you'd probably think of it as a fairly unimportant object among the wonders of space. After all it looks so tiny for a star. But scientists tell us, that because of the closeness of the atoms within the white dwarf, these stars generate a temperature vastly hotter than our own sun.

The white dwarfs are recent discoveries in astronomy and we still know very little about them. They're so far away that we might never be able to voyage anywhere near them. And yet they teach us, through the astronomer's telescope, an ancient truth—something we've heard many times before but which we never seem to learn completely. That's simply that we can't judge by immediate perception. First glances are often deceiving. The truth often lies below the obvious surface of appearances. And this is true not only in astronomy and the physical sciences. It's true in the world of personal relationships as well.

Heavenly Father, help us to see below the surface of outward appearance into the mysteries of all you have created. Give us the wisdom never to make hasty judgements on the evidence of first impressions. Amen.

The White Heat of the Technological Revolution

In 1963 Mr Wilson, before he even became Prime Minister, said that the country was about to be transformed by what he called 'The White Heat of the Technological Revolution'. The kinds of things he had in mind were modern factories making all sorts of useful and entertaining gadgets. And, of course, machines would make life much better for ordinary folk by taking the drudgery out of everyday life.

If you've ever stayed the weekend with someone who has a dish washer you'll appreciate the value of machines. Mr Wilson's miracle hasn't really come true. We've had the oil crisis and an economic slump. But we can at least try and imagine what kind of place the world would have been if the technological revolution had come about.

Labour saving devices abounding. Pocket calculators for every schoolboy. Cheap cars for all. Perhaps, if we let our imagination run riot, we can imagine moving pavements to save us the trouble of walking and lessons by television to replace the teacher. But this isn't really what Mr Wilson had in mind. He simply pictured a world from which a lot of boring and thankless tasks had been removed.

But what would an automated and mechanized world be like in fact? Maybe a lot of the drabness of everyday existence would be taken away for ever. Perhaps, though, the price would be too high—and not just the economic cost—but the price in terms of human happiness.

Imagine for a moment not Mr Wilson's world, but the technological revolution gone mad. All the soul or spirit would've disappeared. Even endless ease and leisure is too high a ransom to pay for our lives being run by gadgets.

A man called Arthur Koestler once suggested that men and women need an almost indefinable 'untied up' dimension to life: what he called a 'Ghost in the Machine'—a part of the world that's not entirely predictable. A part responsible for surprises and newness. Maybe the white heat of the technological revolution would make living much easier but at the cost of making life itself uninteresting.

Heavenly Father, thankyou for newness and differences. We're glad that no two days are exactly alike. Help us to respond to the challenge of each new morning. Amen.

White Lies

Once there was a boy about eleven years old. His grandma, a kindly old lady but quite frail now and in her eighties, had made him a custard pie. Now this lad was very fond of his grandma and she of him. But he was even more fond, if that were possible, of custard pies.

So after a day spent at grandma's house Peter took the custard pie home and ate a good sized portion of it at teatime. Not being a completely mean boy, he gave some to his sister and his mother. Dad didn't like custard pies very much.

The following day, Peter, sister and mum were violently sick. But dad wasn't. It seemed fair to conclude, all things taken into consideration, that the cause was the custard pie. Anyway as the day went on they became well again and forgot all about the incident. They forgot until Saturday that is, when Peter was due to visit grandma again.

'Don't say a word to grandma about the effect of that pie,' said mum.

'But what if she asks?' replied Peter. 'I'll be forced to say something and I can't tell lies can I?'

'Well, it's a white lie', his mother said. 'A white lie is when you tell an untruth for a good reason.'

Sure enough, if Peter had told grandma that the pie had made them ill the old lady would have been terribly upset. But if he hadn't told her, perhaps she, being old, might have made the same mistake in the next pie she'd made and maybe poisoned herself.

Anyway if we're suddenly told that not all untruths are lies—that there are such things as 'white lies', where's it all going to stop? How can we tell when we're right not to tell the truth? Might it not lead to everyone simply telling lies when it suited him? Then we'd be in a mess. No one would believe anyone else. But if Peter had said the pie wasn't delicious he'd perhaps needlessly upset an old lady whose one remaining pleasure was to bake the occasional treat for her grandchildren.

This is just to say that it's very difficult to lay down absolute rules of behaviour, saying *this* is always right and *that* is always wrong. But for everybody's sake there have to be rules. You might like to think of what these rules should be.

Heavenly Father, help us in those situations when we have to make very difficult decisions and where it looks as though whatever we do we'll be in the wrong. Amen.

Name Index

Theme Index

Subject Index